COINS
⁂ OF THE
BIBLE

Written by
Arthur L. Friedberg

Whitman
Publishing, LLC
PUBLISHING SINCE 1934

Art Direction: Matthew W. Jeffirs
Book Design: Jennifer Williams
Editor: Teresa Lyle

Photography generously provided by Leu Numismatics, William M. Rosenblum

and Dr. James Troglen.

ISBN 0794819168

TABLE OF CONTENTS

INTRODUCTION

They are two of the oldest and most recognizable subjects imaginable: money and the Bible. Each has a history of thousands of years, has universal familiarity, and is held dear by multitudes the world over, admittedly with varying degrees of fervor and commitment from time to time and place to place.

Why then another book about two subjects so transparently familiar? Even the combination of the two has been the subject of many other works during the past century and a half. Some have been thin and direct, others impressive tomes encompassing hundreds of pages. Why do it? Because interest in the story, in all of its respects, remains as strong as it has ever been. The Bible in 2004 is still a current event and a best seller. As for coins, of the many books written on the subject, many are over a century old. There are, of course, some marvelous books of recent vintage, those by David Hendin, Ya'akov Meshorer, and others, which are excellent sources for the serious collector and should be a part of any numismatic library of consequence. Many of these titles, however, are beyond the scope, interest, and budget of a reader with a numismatic interest more borne of biblical and historic curiosity than detailed scientific investigation. It is for this latter reader that this book is intended.

The Bible is one of the historical documents available to the historian to help describe the events of the past and enable him or her to draw conclusions from them. But history's resources are not confined only to those items on a bookshelf. Equally important in helping analyze and define the past are contemporary documents, that is, those produced during the period of study.

When you think of the Holy Land, for instance, the first documents that come to mind are probably the Bible and the Dead Sea Scrolls. But there are other historical documents as well. An archaeologist would strongly agree. So would a numismatist (a student of coins). Some could argue that the most important documents of all are the coins made during the times I discuss. Each of them, and there are many, is a historic document in itself. They are thousands of years old, sometimes showing the ravages of time, but sometimes, through the good fortune of having been secreted away to be discovered millennia later, in pristine condition. They are sometimes dull and corroded, but other times gleaming with brilliance. Who can imagine what stories each of these coins has to tell? Where has it been? Who, two thousand years ago, patrician or pauper, held it and passed it along the wheel of commerce? What did the coin buy? Was there a Roman soldier who perhaps took it for his daily pay? Imagine the stories that each of these treasured tiny documents may tell, and which, for too long, have been ignored by too many. In the pages that follow, read some of those stories.

INTRODUCTION

This primer is not meant to be a complete guide to the coins found in the Bible or to the coins that circulated in the Holy Land. What this book will do is give the reader a taste of what numismatics can bring to the table. Perhaps, also, it will serve as the encouragement needed to embark on the pursuit of a lifetime: coin collecting.

In the following section, there is a brief descriptive history of the Holy Land. It is important to know this, so that you will later be able to understand the coins in their historical context. One of the most important things you will discover, and its importance should not be underestimated, is that for most of its history, the Holy Land was rarely an independent political entity. It was instead a colony with degrees of autonomy, varying from self-governing in nearly all respects to complete subjugation. This history of foreign domination was reflected in its coins as much as it was politically, socially, and economically.

You will see how each coin reflects the politics of its time. The coins will be presented in a mostly chronological order. It would take many hundreds of pages, far more than in this book, to present a comprehensive catalog of the coinage. This is rather a compendium of the money of biblical times, consisting mostly of those coins that I have concluded would be most significant in the eyes of the reader.

Some of them are coins that are specifically mentioned in the New Testament. In those cases, there is the biblical text referring to them, so you can place them in their scriptural context. Other coins are not mentioned specifically in the Bible but are known by inference and logic that they circulated in the Holy Land and were part of its economic life. Indeed, I should point out that no coins are mentioned in the Old Testament. In fact, coinage began no earlier than the time period of the Old Testament's last books. Denominations such as the shekel and the talent, for example, initially signified a specific weight, rather than a coin.

Following the section on the coins is a timeline in which the coins are placed in a historical perspective.

AN HISTORIC RETROSPECTIVE
OF THE HOLY LAND

AN HISTORIC RETROSPECTIVE
OF THE HOLY LAND

The Holy Land. It is part of what is generally called the "Cradle of Civilization," and it is as old as time itself. It is small in size, and most of it has never been an idyllic "Land of Milk and Honey." In fact, it is rather an inhospitable, mountainous, arid, and usually hot region. You may wonder why so many battles have been fought over what logic would dictate, based on size, population, and economic output should be an inconsequential part of the world. Instead, it has played a part in history far out of proportion to any reasonable standard of measure. Some ancient mapmakers even considered it the center of their flat world. Could it be that its location was advantageous in some respects? After all, it was at the center of trade routes and was at the edge of three continents–Asia, Europe and Africa--and at the eastern end of the Mediterranean, the most important body of water in the world until the time of the Portuguese navigators in the 15th century.

Perhaps, but these physical and economic benefits are not all that makes it hold such significance. What is important is that it became the home for three religions rooted in the concept of monotheism: Judaism, Christianity, and Islam.

Canaan and the Kingdoms

The land bridge known in early historic time as the land of Canaan is the site of Jericho, the world's oldest city. By 3,000 B.C., Canaan already had strategic importance as the buffer between the world's two superpowers, the Assyrians to the north and the Egyptians to the south. By virtue of its location, Canaan was, even at this prehistoric date, occupied and settled by numerous successive tribes from the Mediterranean, Africa, and near Asia. They are names familiar to readers of Genesis; among others, they are the original inhabitants, the Amorites, and then the Hittites, Phoenicians, Moabites, and Edomites. Among the new settlers around 2,000 B.C., whom could be classified as Iraqi refugees, was a shepherd named Abraham.

Not long after Abraham arrived, the land became a battlefield for the first of many times when the Hittites invaded from the north to fight the Egyptians and in doing so gave the Canaanites and the children of Abraham a chance to assert themselves in battle.

AN HISTORIC RETROSPECTIVE
OF THE HOLY LAND

To their neighbors, Abraham's nomadic people, the Hebrews, must have been an odd bunch. Whereas "normal" people worshiped and made all forms of sacrifices to different idols responsible for every aspect of their existence, Abraham had something else: a monotheistic "God." This God of Abraham was different from all the others. There was only one of him, he had no physical form, and he was all-powerful.

As nomads or wanderers, the Hebrews found themselves in other parts of the land as well, and eventually they ended up as slaves in Egypt at the time of the great building programs there. This set the stage, about a thousand years after Abraham, for the emergence of another great leader, Moses, who led his people back to the promised land of Canaan. After the death of Moses, the Hebrew reconquest of Canaan was a gradual one. At first they controlled only the area east of the Jordan River and some additional mountainous territory. Another tribe, the Philistines, remained in control of the Mediterranean coast.

The twelve tribes of Israel settled into a designated area of the "promised land." Their first leaders were the "Judges." They led the tribes during a time of nearly constant battle with the pagan natives. Towards the end of second millennium B.C., it was clear that a unifying force, a king, was needed to unify the tribes against their enemies, lead an army, and much like America in the days after the Revolution, be the head of a strong central government.

The judge and prophet Samuel was pressured by the people to select such a man, and he chose Saul. It turned out to be a prophetic choice. Saul was a fierce warrior as was one of his commanders, his son Jonathan. During thirty-six years of war, he created a standing army and was able to prevail in combat more often than not. In fact, perhaps his greatest enemy was not a military one, but the man to whom he owed his position, Samuel.

Nonetheless, he left a strong foundation for his successor, King David. Centuries before the Renaissance, King David was the world's first Renaissance man. A shepherd, David became an epic warrior, psalmist, statesman, king, and founder of the holy city of Jerusalem. It has been said that David's greatest decision was also one of the most important ever made for mankind. In about 1,004 B.C., in his first major act after becoming king, he brought the Ark of the Covenant, built in the Sinai by Moses and containing the tablets of the Ten Commandments, to Jerusalem.

The first mention of Jerusalem ("Ursalim") is found on some Egyptian pottery known as the Execration Texts from c. 1,850 B.C. Abraham visited Jerusalem twice, one of those times to be tested with the binding of Isaac on Mt. Moriah. Otherwise, it was mostly just another Canaanite settlement, and there's little mention of it until David's time. By proclaiming it his capital, David had a central and neutral location from which he could extend his power and exert his control. Similar to Washington D.C. today, which is a capital city outside the control of the fifty states, Jerusalem was David's capital outside the control of the twelve tribes.

During his forty-year reign, David achieved the ultimate victory over the Philistines and gained controlling access to the Mediterranean. He defeated the Edomites in the southern desert and by doing so extended his power all the way to the Red Sea. He also defeated the Moabites and Ammonites in what is now Jordan and the people of Aram from present day eastern Syria. His realm extended as far north as Damascus, and in the east, all the way to the Euphrates River. It is important to note that the only cities that remained independent were some Philistine enclaves in the south, and especially some Phoenician cities in what is now Lebanon. One of those cities, Tyre became an important trading partner and ally. It was with the help of King Hiram of Tyre that David was able to acquire the technical expertise and building materials necessary for the construction of his palace.

Solomon, the son of David and Bathsheba and heir to the throne, consolidated his father's gains and made an alliance with Egypt. The kingdom of Israel was in its Golden Age. Its empire was expansive, it was domestically centralized, and its commerce flourished with trading colonies established far afield. Solomon even replaced military force with diplomacy (which included the taking of at least dozens of wives from places both practical and exotic). Solomon also doubled the size of Jerusalem and selected Mt. Moriah as the sight of the Holy Temple.

The construction and completion of the Temple remains one of the crowning glories in the history of the children of Israel. It was Solomon's obsession, and to complete it, he instituted a policy of "tax and spend." He raised taxes, imported slaves, imposed forced labor on tens of thousands, and put his government into debt. Even with all that, the Temple could never have been completed without the Phoenicians, to whom Solomon amassed so much indebtedness that he had to pay King Hiram back not only with goods, but also with territory. From Phoenicia came knowledge in the form of engineers, artisans, craftsmen, and raw materials such as the famous cedars of Lebanon.

AN HISTORIC RETROSPECTIVE
OF THE HOLY LAND

With the end of King Solomon's forty-year reign came the end of the united Jewish state. The first three kings of the Jews were able to manage, through power and ingenuity, to keep the rancor between the twelve tribes in check. Without strong leadership ability, Solomon's successors were not so fortunate. Solomon was oppressive and prejudiced towards the ten northern tribes but he was able to contain them. After his passing, the result was secession and civil war. The ten northern tribes united to form the kingdom of Israel while the tribes of Judah and Benjamin continued the lineage of the house of David and formed the kingdom of Judah with Jerusalem as its capital. For the next two hundred years, from about 928 to 722 B.C., the small kingdoms existed as neighbors and often rivals, but united when it came to the importance of Jerusalem.

Judea had terrible land for farming, lost its commercial capabilities and its access to the best trade routes, was deserted by skilled labor, and saw its military power diminish. Fortunately, the legacy of David's dynasty gave it a degree of domestic stability that was lacking in the north. But it was a tempting target and the Egyptians, who, emboldened by the weakness of the new leaders, attacked Jerusalem. The city was saved by using the Temple's treasure to bribe the conquering army. Jerusalem, then as now, was a unifying force for the people of the land. Under the reign of King Asa (908-867 B.C.), the paganism and idol worship that had been creeping its way back into daily life was eradicated, and many from the north joined their southern cousins in returning to observe the Hebrew rituals in the Temple.

Economically, the northern kingdom of Israel tended to dominate. Spiritually, however, it was in chaos. Palace revolts and usurpations were the norm. A strong king named Omri emerged and was called "David of the North." He succeeded in restoring order and some respect for authority. He further strengthened ties with Phoenicia and built a new capital city, said to have been even more beautiful than Jerusalem, which he called "Samaria." Omri's son, Ahab, expanded the land territorially but allowed it to be plundered morally. His wife was a Phoenician princess and the daughter of the king of Sidon. The ignominy that comes with her name, Jezebel, was well earned when she brought the worship of the idol Baal to the court of the Jews. Before Jezebel met her destiny at the jaws of a pack of mad dogs, she precipitated one of the great battles of good versus evil. On the side of the former came the prophet Elijah. He was the first of a series of great prophets who would serve as beacons of rectitude for a people being torn way from their roots and whose moral teachings still bear relevance today.

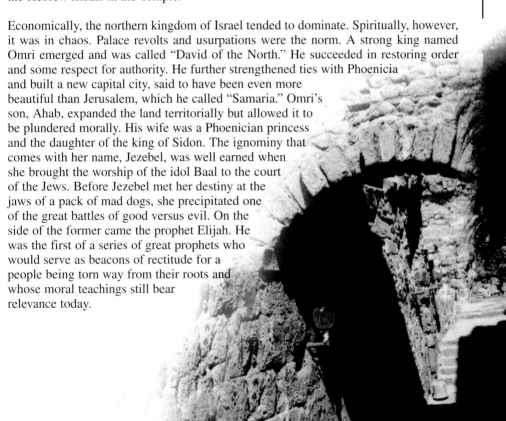

In those days, however, the task was more immediate: the need to eliminate the threat posed by Baal. By the middle of the ninth century B.C., the task was completed in both kingdoms. Unfortunately, the price was that the people were too drained from the years of internal strife to fight any longer. A victorious internal battle gave way to one to be lost to outsiders. The gates opened for a successful Assyrian invasion and soon after that a more brutal conquest by the Aram-Damascus Syrians. This was the end of the northern kingdom. Alliances were necessary to survive so Israel joined with Aram-Damascus. After a three-year war, the city of Samaria was conquered in 722 B.C., and many of the kingdom of Israel's residents were sent into exile. This was the beginning of what is known today as the "Diaspora." There is still no way of tracing what became of those ten "lost" tribes.

Rather than fight, the kingdom of Judah opted for appeasement with the invaders, and by forming this alliance, along with several others, it was able to survive for another century and a half. Its position as a crossroads did it more harm than good. There was rebellion throughout the Assyrian Empire. Hordes of Scythians laid waste to both Syria and Palestine, and by about 600 B.C., the occupying Assyrians were replaced by the Babylonians under King Nebuchadnezzar. The Judeans saw this as their time to revolt, thinking they could exploit the fact that Babylon was mired in a war with Egypt. They even counted on Egyptian help (which never materialized). Nebuchadnezzar struck back and overran the country. In 586 B.C., he destroyed Solomon's temple, and by 581 B.C. had burned Jerusalem to the ground. Most of the population was sent into exile, many to Babylonia, which ironically became a center of Jewish learning and where, as long as they did not agitate, the Jews were allowed to prosper.

When Nebuchadnezzar died, Babylon found itself facing an enemy unlike any it had seen before: the great Persian Empire, which stretched from India to Greece. Babylon sat right in the middle of it and Persia's King Cyrus decided it had to go.

Cyrus handily defeated the Babylonians and in 538 B.C. issued an edict allowing the return of the exiles to Judah. Within a century, despite misery and distrustful residents such as the Samaritans (residents of Samaria) all around them, they rebuilt Jerusalem's walls and restored the Temple. This story is told in the books of Nehemiah and Ezra. It suffices to say that this led to a rebirth of life for the land of Judah. Although under the kings of Persia, it was a small and relatively insignificant province, it flourished and had a bearable degree of freedom in language, religion, and domestic affairs. It saw the

rise of a great power to the West, Athens. Next, from the North came one of the most lionized leaders of all time, and a man who permanently changed not only the face of the Holy Land, but also of the entire Mediterranean world, Alexander the Great of Macedon. So begins the story of nine centuries of the Holy Land as part of the Greco-Roman worlds.

Greek Judea

The reign of Alexander the Great was brief (336-323 B.C.) in duration but monumental in significance. In 333 B.C., he conquered Syria and moved to Egypt where he established the city of Alexandria a year later. In the Holy Land, much of the population adopted the Hellenistic lifestyle. Even Jerusalem got its own gymnasiums, temples, and Greek forms of entertainment. But the area remained autonomous and religious freedom continued for those who so chose. The Hebrew scriptures were even translated into Greek.

After the death of Alexander, the area again became an object of dispute between the forces of Seleucus, the Macedonian general who took over control in the east, and Ptolemy, the founder of the dynasty of that name in Egypt. It fell to the latter in about 301 B.C., but in 198 B.C. the Egyptians were defeated by the forces of the Seleucid King Antiochus III (223-187 B.C.)

His son and successor, Antiochus Epiphanes IV, did not view tolerance as a virtue. He chose to "Hellenize" everything. He ordered the sacrifice of pigs in the Holy Temple and reconsecrated it in honor of Zeus. Pillage and debauchery became *de rigeur*. It had the encouragement and active participation of a good portion of the population, who gleefully and willingly welcomed the more hedonistic and self-indulgent lifestyle. With this, some of the other Jews had seen enough and began a war of resistance that is known as the Revolt of the Maccabees.

The Maccabees, also known as the Hasmoneans, were members of the priestly family of patriarch (Matthias) and his five sons, the eldest and leader being Judah (Judas Macca-beus in Latin). For four years, they conducted a guerilla war of such tactical brilliance that even four progressively larger reinforcements of the Seleucid garrisons had no effect. The Maccabees retook and rededicated the Temple in 164 B.C.(much more detail on this event may be found in the story of the Jewish Hanukkah festival). The armies remained stalemated for another two decades as Judea became stabilized and settled under Hasmonean rule for the next century.

The ablest and youngest of the Maccabee brothers was Simon, who assumed command after Judah was killed. He convinced the Roman Senate to recognize Judean independence and in 142 B.C, finally received the same acknowledgment from the Seleucids. In 140 B.C., the Maccabees were given the dual responsibilities of the monarchy and the priesthood. For the next hundred years, the Hasmonean dynasty restored Judea to a position not seen since the days of Solomon. Still, Hellenization was not abandoned, particularly culturally. For example, many Jews, even the kings, took on additional Greek names.

For the Judeans, this interlude was probably too good to be true. The internecine struggles resumed as in the days of the two kingdoms. One of the first tasks of John Hyrcanus (Yehohanan, 135-104 B.C.), Simon's sole surviving son and immediate successor, was to put down an attempted coup by his brother-in-law. He next had to thwart an attempted invasion by the Seleucids, led by Antiochus VII Sidetes, by which he (according to Flavius Josephus) raided King David's tomb and plundered it of 3,000 talents of silver. He took a tenth of it to bribe Antiochus to lift his siege and used the balance to hire mercenaries to fight with him in the future. Hyrcanus exploited the opportunities available to him by retaking parts of Judea across the Jordan River and Samaria in the north and east and in the south by beating the Edomites (known more familiarly as Idumaea).

Successes aside, another tempest was brewing which would dwarf any temporary military glory. John Hyrcanus was the creator of a group of elders and judges known as the Sanhedrin. They were drawn from the segment of the population one today would call the "haves." It was ostensibly their job to protect the people and the law, but in reality, their mission was to protect the status quo inside and outside the Temple and to legitimatize the king's actions. This did not sit well with a rising opposition among some segments of the people to the rampant Hellenism that the authorities condoned. A group that would become known as the "Pharisees," (from the Hebrew word for "separate") began to question the political and economic conservatism of the rule. While religious, they were not opposed to change, and they "radically" proposed that the law (the Hebrew Torah) was subject to interpretation and revision. They would eventually advocate in their piety and their teachings a stricter interpretation of the traditional law. At the time of Hyrcanus' death, however, they just represented a difference of opinion.

AN HISTORIC RETROSPECTIVE
OF THE HOLY LAND

John's first son, Judah Aristobulus (Yehuda) ruled for only one year and was succeeded by his brother, Alexander Jannaeus (Yehonatan), who, from 103-76 B.C., with nearly constant battle, succeeded in reuniting the entire Holy Land for the first time since David and Solomon. But his domestic programs had the opposite effect: they divided. Jannaeus was so profane that the Pharisees rose up in civil war and even had the hated Seleucids come in and help overthrow their own king! They prevailed in battle but then had second thoughts about the Syrians. Both sides proceeded to a reconciliation of sorts, which was briefly cemented by Jannaeus' wife and successor, Queen Salome Alexandra. In fact, the balance of power had shifted to the Pharisees.

Alexandra, whose reign lasted from 76-67 B.C., had two sons, the weak John Hyrcanus II (Yonatan), whom she named High Priest, and the stronger and younger Judah Aristobulus II, whom she kept quiet. She also named some Pharisees to the Sanhedrin. The two sons did not get along and the younger sided with the sect of the priestly and moneyed classes known as the Saducees. Upon Alexandra's death, Hyrcanus II took the throne, civil war again broke out, and the new king abdicated. Into the breach now stepped an Idumenian named Antipater who controlled just a small area in the south. Antipater was both evil and cunning, and he proposed to help Hyrcanus. The two went to the Nabataean King Aretas, who pledged assistance on the condition that he be ceded the land southeast of the Dead Sea. Their forces then began to march on Jerusalem.

It is astounding to think that the Romans were actually invited into the land that they would soon completely subjugate, but that is what happened next.

The Roman Conquest

Roman forces under their famous general Pompey (the Great) were already in the Middle East and had just captured Damascus. In Jerusalem, the two sons were at war. Pompey had the dual task of expanding the Roman territories and reviving Hellenism. He sent his general Scaurus to Judea with orders to bring hostilities to a halt. As soon as he arrived, both sides asked him for aid. After some negotiation and not a small bit of bribery and intrigue, Pompey called both sides to Damascus. There he finally decided to throw his might behind the weaker Hyrcanus II. The forces of Aristobulus resisted and took up refuge on Jerusalem's Temple grounds.

And so in 63 B.C., into the city of Jerusalem marched the legions of Pompey, its gates opened wide for them by none other than Hyrcanus II. The siege lasted three months and thousands were killed. As his reward, Pompey reappointed John Hyrcanus II as High Priest, a position he held until 40 B.C. His henchman Antipater was made Administrator-General of Judea. Antipater had two sons, each of whom he appointed prefects (governors). To Phasael he gave Jerusalem. To the other, Herod, he awarded Galilee.

If Herod's family had been the Maccabees, he would probably have been viewed differently. No matter what he did, he was detested by the Jews. To the Romans, however, he would be an answer to their prayers. After the murder of Caesar in 44 B.C., Rome had its own squabbles to settle. Sensing an opportunity, the remnants of the Hasmonean party tried to take advantage of an anarchic situation. The son of Aristobulus II, Mattathias Antigonus lured Rome's hated Parthian rivals into invading with the object of replacing his uncle Hyrcanus II as High Priest. For three years, until 37 B.C., he had his wish and the support of a majority of the people. Herod in the meantime fled to Masada and then to Rome.

As far as the Romans were concerned, the Judean throne was vacant. Hyrcanus II was incapable and could not be restored anyway. His adversary, Antigonus, was considered a usurper. Herod was already well known among the powers in Rome for his earlier activities. Marc Antony and Octavian (later known as Emperor Augustus) proposed, and the Roman Senate concurred in 40 B.C., to name Herod the new King of Judea.

For the next three years, Herod would be king, as far as Rome was concerned, while Antigonus remained in control of Jerusalem. Finally, with the help of a large influx of Roman legions, Herod took Jerusalem in 37 B.C. after a five-month siege. Most of the opposition, including Antigonus and nearly the entire Sanhedrin, was beheaded. From 37 B.C. to A.D. 4, Herod and his policies framed the world into which Jesus was born.

Rome rewarded Herod handsomely. It gave him extra territory, so that his dominion included nearly the entire land of Israel. He, in turn, built defenses and became the personification of Roman policy and culture. He "rehellenized" the territory and consolidated it politically and economically. He built some magnificent new cities, the most

famous of which is undoubtedly Caesarea. Herod considered himself a Jew, though by nature of his birth, he was not entitled to the priesthood. As in other Roman colonies, he allowed and encouraged the continued practice of the local religion and to that end, and in an effort to gain public support, he completely rebuilt the Holy Temple. It became one of the most imposing structures of its day, and the equal, it is said, of the great edifices of Greece and Rome. To further secure power, he appointed a weak leader by the name of Hananel to the post of High Priest.

There is a famous quote from the Emperor Augustus, with ample historical justification in the stories of how Herod treated people, saying: *Melius est Herodis porcum esse quam filium* ("It is better to be Herod's pig than his son.") All the bricks, mortar, marble, gold, and silver could not mask the tempest brewing among the people. The New Testament covers his reign in great detail.

The Jews remained divided about nearly everything except their contempt for Herod. They were still split into the Sadducees who, to preserve their own role, perpetuated the status quo in the Temple and leaned towards compromise with the Romans (note: this is the same view as that of the "Herodian Party" in the New Testament though in a less Hellenistic direction); and the Pharisees, who offered a more rigorous interpretation of the law of the Bible and whose outlook was more geared towards the masses. There were now two more groups: the Essenes, about whom so much has been learned, after the discovery of the Dead Sea Scrolls at Qumran in 1947. They seem to have been a group of renegade Hasmoneans that fled Jerusalem in the time of Alexander Jannaeus and set up a commune-type facility in the desert. They may have returned to Jerusalem in the time of Herod, but fled again soon thereafter. They had two core beliefs: 1) that the end of the world was approaching and the biblical prophecy of the Messiah was about to be fulfilled, and 2) that they were the predestined ones that God had chosen to save the world and that they would be in turn saved by God in the end. Finally, there were the Zealots, a group of wild radicals that advocated the violent overthrow of the Roman occupation.

Towards the end of Herod's reign, palace intrigues spun so out of control that Herod even had three of his sons executed. He outraged the populace even more by placing a Roman eagle at the Temple entrance. At his death in 4 B.C., any efforts he had made to appease the Jews could be regarded as nothing but resounding failures. His death sparked a series of revolts, which could only be suppressed by the Roman army. The problem of succession was settled by Augustus, who followed Herod's will and spilt the territory among Herod's three surviving sons. None got the title of king. To Herod Archelaus he gave the title "Ethnarch" (head of nation) and Judea and Samaria, including Caesarea and the other cities along the coast.

Herod Antipas received Galilee and an area across the Jordan River. He built the city of Tiberius. The Herod of the New Testament, who put John the Baptist to death, is Antipas, not Herod the Great. Herod Philip received some primarily non-Jewish areas in what is now Jordan and was by all accounts an effective ruler. The two latter sons were called "Tetrarchs" (a lesser title than Ethnarch). Archelaus lasted just nine years and was sent to Gaul in A.D. 6. Antipas was ousted by Caligula in A.D. 39 and Philip died of natural causes in A.D. 34.

The Procurators of Judea

After Herod Archelaus was exiled to Gaul, Rome annexed Judea to the province of Syria. The Jewish revolts and uprisings were continuing and required a stronger hand. Rome instituted rule by a series of governors who were initially called "prefects" and later "procurators." They established their capital in Herod's Caesarea and were responsible for collecting taxes, appointing high priests, and asserting control. There is dispute among sources as to whether they tried to avoid provoking the community or took relish in it. As with all humanity, there were some good and some bad among the fourteen procurators who served from A.D. 6 to 66. But there is no dispute that most of them were low-level officials unfit for the job. Their control of the province was only interrupted by the kingship of Herod Agrippa I from A.D. 37-44. He received the title as a reward from his patron, the notorious Emperor Caligula.

There is no need to go into the very-well told story of Jesus. It should suffice to understand his environment. Jesus' brief life on earth occurred on a landscape of bewildering chaos. Tiberius became Emperor and served from A.D. 14 to 37. He was enjoying a life of debauchery too much at his villa in Capri to have any concerns about a small and insignificant far away province. The Jewish people were in a near constant state of turmoil and were looking for the promised coming of the Messiah. The worse things got, the harder the Jews looked to find their messiah. The tax collections were becoming onerous, and the Zealots started a revolt that lived up to their name and which was only put down by a pair of legions sent from Syria.

As if this were not bad enough, Tiberius then appointed Pontius Pilate as Procurator. This was a man completely ignorant of the people he was to govern and about as cruel and revolting a figure as the human imagination can conceive. First and foremost, it must be remembered that he was a politician whose most important job was to please Rome. He raided the Holy Treasury for funds to build an aqueduct, thinking the Jews would be grateful. He blasphemed the city of Jerusalem by placing busts of the Emperor on his military standards, something even his predecessors knew better than to do.

He put Roman priestly implements on his coins instead of the traditional symbols (although this was probably through ignorance rather than malice).

There were similarities between the ideas of Essenes and the teachings of John the Baptist. How close they may have been and whether they interacted with each other is not relevant except to show that the area was ready for another line of religious thought, one of ethical standards, charity, humility, and brotherly love. It was into this void that Jesus and the disciples stepped. It is clear that His teachings would have appealed more to the commoners than the privileged and the Pharisees. One can understand how John the Baptist, with his concepts of piety and divine judgment, would have affected Herod Antipas in the Galilee, and how Jesus would have had to flee and preach elsewhere until things calmed down. It is no surprise that the new group would be a haven for those disaffected from the Saducees, Pharisees, Herodians, and others.

Neither should the reaction they received when they reached Jerusalem be a surprise: not the reaction of the masses in the Temple and the political impact Jesus had; not the betrayal by Judas; not the apprehension by the High Priest's constables; not the alleged charge of blasphemy by a Sanhedrin that had been stripped of most of its power and legal capacity, and certainly not the sentence of Pontius Pilate, imposed in the name of Rome, clearly for political reasons.

Pilate remained procurator until A.D. 36. He was finally recalled and made to stand trial on charges of failing to administer justice properly. His conduct was too monstrous even for the Romans.

The time after the crucifixion, with little exception, was a period of insurrection and anarchy. The beginning of the end came when Caligula decided to have his image put in the Temple. Fortunately, he was assassinated before things exploded. The experience showed how susceptible the colony was to Roman whims and strengthened the hand of the extremist factions.

The rule of Herod Agrippa, (A.D. 37-44), who was restored to the throne by the new emperor Claudius as a gesture of appreciation for his assistance, was good for the Jews, with whom he was popular, and bad for the Christians, whom he persecuted.

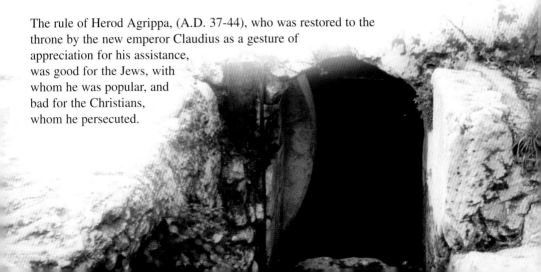

Overall, his reign was too brief to have any lasting effect. Claudius felt Agrippa II, the son, was too young to reign and so he reinstituted the role of the procurators. By the reign of Nero (A.D. 54-68), these later procurators were administering the province in a manner that ranks as a shining star in the annals of incompetence. The structure of society was torn apart by civil unrest and class warfare. Even the Pharisees joined the Zealots in calling for a revolt against Rome.

The First Revolt of the Jews lasted from A.D. 66-70. At first, the rebels racked up a number of impressive successes and had the effect of turning a rebellion into a bona fide war. Rome was threatened; it no longer viewed Judea as an unimportant outpost. First, the loss of any territory was unacceptable. Second, it would cut off the land route between the major Roman cities of Antioch in the north and Alexandria in the south. In A.D. 67, Nero gave the governorship of Judea to his general there, the future emperor Vespasian. For the first couple of years of the campaign, the rebellion even brought a degree of independent self-government back to the Jews. But the power of Vespasian's legions, said to number about 60,000 men, began to turn the tide, albeit slowly. Step by step and city by city, they retook the province. Only the city of Jerusalem and a few reinforced outposts remained free.

The battle for Jerusalem was long and bloody. It was a fight not only with Rome but also with rival factions within the city. It did not end until after Vespasian had already returned to Rome to become emperor and turned his Judean army over to his son Titus. By the spring of A.D. 70, Titus had four legions (80,000 troops) at his disposal against 25,000 defenders holding the high ground. Titus opted to starve the city first and attack it later. This he did after a few months, and on the ninth day of the Hebrew month of Av, the Romans entered the Temple, pillaged its contents, and burned it down. The whole city fell under imperial control within a month. The desert fortress of Masada and its thousand defenders held out for another three years.

After that a great many inhabitants were sent into exile. Others remained, both in the city of Jerusalem and more particularly in Galilee where, with the acquiescence of

Rome, a reconstituted Sanhedrin had its seat. Rome again reverted to a laissez-faire policy concerning internal affairs, though under Domitian (A.D. 81-96) Roman troops were posted in the province permanently, and the governor was a Roman senator rather than a lowly procurator. Domitian also imposed a tax known as a tribute only on Jews. This was rescinded by his successor Nerva (A.D. 96-98).

The reign of Trajan (A.D. 98-117) began in tranquility and remained so until near the end of his reign. At that time, rebellions outside Judea led to retribution for the sake of order within. The emperor Hadrian (A.D. 117-138) visited the remnants of Jerusalem in A.D. 130 and while there decided to rebuild it as the Roman city of Aelia Capitolina. He then proceeded to renege on promises to lower taxes and modify some laws and instituted yet another Hellenization program that included outlawing circumcision, reading the Torah, and observing the Sabbath. This was the spark that set off the Second Jewish Revolt.

It was helpful to the revolt that Akiva, a great rabbi of the day, chose to announce that the Messiah had come. Akiva said it was Simon Bar-Kochba (Simon, the son of a star), based on a biblical phrase: "There shall come a star out of Jacob." (Numbers 24: 17) Behind the latest messiah, the nation massed an army of at least 200,000 and rallied. As in the First Revolt, the initial victories were numerous. The Roman governor had to flee, and the Jews reestablished their own government under Bar-Kochba. A large portion of the land outside Galilee came under their control. Bar-Kochba's messianic pretensions did little to endear him to the new small sect known as Christians, upon whom he retaliated vengeance for their disloyalty.

The arrival of the general Julius Severus from Britain in A.D. 134 changed the tide. Severus and his massive force embarked on a two-year war of attrition resulting in horrific casualties on both sides. Finally, Jerusalem surrendered and Aelia Capitolina rejoined the empire. Bar-Kochba and his remaining followers fled to the fortress city of Bethar outside Jerusalem where they were killed in the summer of A.D. 135. As for the other consequences: 50 fortresses and 985 villages were destroyed. The name of the province became Syria Palaestina (Palestine, after the Philistines). On the people, Hadrian unleashed a program of revenge perhaps without equal even in the blood thirsty history of Rome. Scholars were tortured to death, captives were auctioned into slavery, and refugees massed in the ports. Jews became a minority everywhere except in Galilee. It was forbidden for any remaining Jew to even set foot in Aelia Capitolina, a ban that lasted for about three hundred years until it was lifted by the Empress Eudocia. By that time, Jerusalem had effectively become a Christian city. There would not be another independent Jewish state for almost 1,900 years.

HISTORICAL MAPS
AND LANDSCAPES OF THE BIBLE

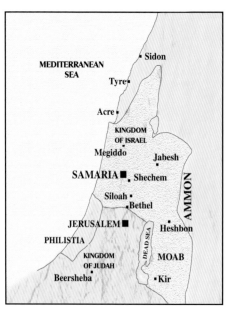

Israel and Judah

722 B.C. Assyrians invade northern kingdom of Israel and inhabitants flee. 586 B.C. Babylonians invade southern kingdom of Judah.

Roman Province

63 B.C. Romans invade and occupy Jerusalem.

LANDSCAPES OF THE BIBLE

Fertile Plain

The narrow western coastal plain extends 117 miles and has beautiful beaches and there citrus crops are grown on the fertile land.

Jordan River

The freshwater of the Jordan River is approximately 64 square miles, and this is where Jesus was baptized: *"Not long afterwards Jesus came from Nazareth and was baptized by John in the Jordan"* (Mark: 1: 9).

Desert

The Negev Desert in the South has dunes and a low-running mountain range that runs from northeast to the southwest. Mount Ramon is the highest mountain at 3,396 feet.

Dead Sea

The lowest point on earth is the surface of the Dead Sea, which is 50 miles long, extending from the Jordan River, and 11 miles wide, with a salt content of anywhere from 25-32 percent, depending on the source, and it's estimated that it is six times more salty than regular ocean water. It is the site of the biblical cities of Sodom and Gomorrah.

THE COINAGE OF BIBLICAL TIMES

Money Before Coinage

The Old Testament is full of references to terms such as skekel and its components, the bekah (half shekel), pim (third shekel), rebah (quarter shekel), gerah (twentieth shekel), and talent. None of these, when mentioned in the earliest of biblical books, refers to coins, which did not exist until much later. When we see these so-called denominations, they are always referring to a particular weight of precious metal.

Some examples:

Genesis 24: 22 "... *the man took a golden earring of half a shekel weight, and two bracelets for her hands of ten shekels weight of gold.*"

Exodus 38: 26 "*A bekah for every man, that is, half a shekel ...*"

Exodus 38: 27 "*And of the hundred talents of silver were cast the sockets of the sanctuary.*"

Nehemiah 10: 33 "*Also we made ordinances for us, to charge ourselves yearly with the third part of a shekel for the service of the house of our God.*"

I Samuel 9: 8 "*Behold, I have here at hand the fourth part of a shekel of silver: that I will give to the man of God, to tell us our way.*"

Exodus 30: 13 "*This they shall give, every one that passeth, among them that are numbered, half a shekel after the shekel of the sanctuary: (a shekel is twenty gerahs:) an half shekel shall be the offering of the Lord.*"

The first portion quoted above is especially significant because it shows that even in the time of Abraham precious metal was already considered a form of portable wealth and a measure of value. There is no doubt that even in the earliest times it had an important role in trade, but under the barter system, it was not the only measure of value. It could just as easily have been an ox, cow, goat, fish, or anything else that was of surplus value to one party that would be willingly accepted by another. The talent was related in value to an ox. The common financial term "pecuniary" even has its root in the Latin word *pecus* for cattle. In early Babylon, a shekel roughly equaled the equivalent of 180 grains of barley. It was also the equivalent of 1/60 of a mina or manah, which in turn was 1/60 of the biggest weight of all, the talent.

For obvious reasons, barter can only exist at a primitive economic level. Once trade increased and existed between nations and not just villages, a more uniform and recognizable medium of exchange, which would easily be recognized and accepted by diverse parties, became necessary. Precious metals fit the requirement, either as jewelry or as pieces of metal. However, they had to be weighed carefully and their value agreed upon. We see evidence in Egyptian paintings showing transfers of large rings, bracelets, and ingots.

THE COINAGE OF BIBLICAL TIMES

Ring Money, Weighing Money

Here the problems began. Who could guarantee the weight and purity and thus certify the value? Who could weigh each and every piece of metal brought to them? No one. What occurred instead was that official marks were placed on them that testified to their weight and authenticity. Then they could just be counted. In essence, these were the first primitive coins.

The First Coined Money

It is universally agreed that credit for the invention of coins as we commonly understand them goes to the Lydians in the 7th century B.C. They made coins in electrum, a naturally occurring alloy of gold and silver. To guarantee their value, Lydians stamped the head of a lion--the emblem of the king-- on them. By the time of King Croesus (560-546 B.C.), things became more sophisticated when he issued coins called staters in both gold and silver (one gold stater equaled twenty in silver). As coinage spread eastward to Asia Minor and to the Aegean and mainland Greece, this bimetallic system of gold and silver was accepted everywhere.

Croesus, King of Lydia, 561-546 B.C.

Initially, the coins were usually related to a barter item of equal value, such as the aforementioned ox, turtle shell, olive sprig, or cluster of grapes, to name a few. States later began using their emblems or seals and other devices reminiscent of their names. Next, there appeared portraits of gods and goddesses, and lastly, representations of humans.

It also became necessary to have smaller units of value, so fractional denominations were added with the same basic design as on the larger coins.

Finally, different standards of measuring developed, particularly for coins made out of silver. The two that concern us most are the standards of the Babylonian silver shekel, which equated to 1/45 of a mina and the Phoenician silver shekel at 2/135 of a mina.

THE EARLY COINED MONEY
IN THE HOLY LAND

THE EARLY COINED MONEY
IN THE HOLY LAND

PERSIA

"They gave after their ability unto the treasure of the work threescore and one thousand drams of gold, and five thousand pounds of silver, and one hundred priests' garments." (Ezra 2: 69)

Given that the holy land usually under the control of others, it was nearly always the norm for coins from the trading powers and trading partners of the day to be the money of account. It is generally recognized that the Lydian coinage was succeeded by the coins of the Persian Empire. As the book of Ezra coincides with the early days of the Persian Empire, it does not take long for coins to achieve recognition therein. When in 536 B.C., King Cyrus of Persia allowed the Jews to return to Jerusalem, they undoubtedly carried with them some of the world's first coins. By the sixth year of the reign of King Darius in 516 B.C., the Temple was completed. The text from Ezra cited above refers to the contribution made to defray the costs of construction.

The Hebrew text uses (in transliteration) Darcmonim, which is intended to mean the Persian word "Daric," and it takes its name from King Darius. The gold daric, and its counterpart, the silver siglos, are identical in design and were the standard coins of the Persian Empire until its conquest by Alexander the Great. The coins show a running archer with and without a beard, usually carrying a spear or a dagger and a bow. Although King Darius was surely an inspiration for the coin, it is doubtful that the figure is meant to portray any particular king. The reverse was a simple irregular oblong incuse square.

  Darius I, 521-486 B.C. or Xerxes I, 486-465 B.C.
Kings of Persia

The siglos, too, probably has a biblical reference, which we find in Nehemiah (5: 15), albeit as a shekel: *"But the former governors that had been before me were chargeable unto the people, and had taken of them bread and wine, beside forty shekels of silver."*

ATHENS

Not only one of the most famous coins ever made, but also one of the most important is the tetradrachm of Athens. It was by far the most significant coin in the world during the fourth and fifth centuries B.C. It was among the first coins to bear a full design on each side; it was the largest silver coin in existence up to then (tetra = four) by a factor of two; it remains today, particularly when of the highest style, one of the most beautiful coins ever made; and its reputation for full weight and purity carried it to the edges of the known world. It was preferred above any other coin by Greeks

THE EARLY COINED MONEY
IN THE HOLY LAND

and non-Greeks alike. Although it is said that the tetradrachm roughly equaled a week's wages, it was more suited to the export market. The basic unit, the drachm (and the basis for the modern Greek drachma denomination), was divided into six obols. Among the denominations minted for more common use were the 3 obol, 1 and 1/2 obol, obol, 3/4 obol, 1/2 (hemiobol), 3/8 obol and 1/8 obol. Among the most treasured of all coins among elite collectors today is the massive decadrachm (10 drachms), which was issued mainly for non-commercial purposes such as commemorations.

Athens, Tetradrachm, 449-420 B.C.

Athens, Drachm, 350 B.C.

A look at the coin's presence in archaeological finds gives some indication of its traveling ability. Hoards of them have turned up in Egypt, Syria, Sicily, Tunisia, Spain, Iraq, Iran, Afghanistan, and Israel.

So prevalent was the tetradrachm of Athens, that rather than issue coins of their own design, many localities chose instead to copy the style of Athens. According to Barclay Head, Keeper of the British Museum Coin Cabinet at the end of the nineteenth century, this was because the supply of coins from the mint in Athens was not sufficient to satisfy the demand. Imitations in Syria, Persia, Egypt, Arabia, and India are not the only ones known; they are also found in the Holy Land. During the fourth century B.C., these latter coins, in the denominations of one drachm and smaller, were struck along the coast at the mints of Ashkelon, Gaza, and Samaria, and also in Jerusalem.

In most cases, the style of the imitations does not measure up to the artistic level of the Athenian engravers. For historical purposes, however, that is not what sets them apart. There are some very interesting Jerusalem coins that bear the same head of Athena in profile on the obverse and the same owl on the reverse as the originals. But there are two telling and significant alterations on the reverse. The first is the lettering. On the Athenian coins, the city's name is rendered by the Greek letters **A ΘE**. The Jerusalem type replaces them with letters in archaic Hebrew script that corresponded to "YHD." These are known as the "Yehud" coins and is the name the Persians used for Judea.

Jerusalem, 375-350 B.C.

The second interesting change is the inclusion of a lily on these issues. Scholars feel that the lily is a symbol representative of the Temple and is meant to be as symbolic of Jerusalem as the olive branch is for Athens. The use of the lily as a religious symbol occurs on later Judean coins as well.

The coins of Ashkelon, Gaza, and Samaria parallel the Jerusalem coins in many respects. **AΘE** is replaced by the local mint's name, and although the owl was still an important device, other symbols were also used to reflect local themes.

ALEXANDER THE GREAT OF MACEDON

Athens' loss in its lengthy war with Sparta in 406 B.C. was the beginning of what would be a slow decline in her power and influence which coincided with the rise to the north of the Macedonian Empire. By the end of his reign, Macedon's King Philip II (359-336 B.C.) succeeded in exercising dominion over the Greek mainland as the first step on an agenda of imperial conquest. His murder in 336 B.C. left the kingdom in the hands of his twenty-year old son, Alexander the Great.

Phillip II, King of Macedon, 498-454 B.C.

The same year as Alexander claimed his throne, Persia came into the hands of Darius III. Within three years, the final destiny of the Persian Empire was sealed when Alexander and his forces were victorious in the Battle of Issus, overran Phoenicia, and moved on to Jerusalem. There, Alexander must have had an epiphany of sorts. Legend has it that when the warrior-king entered Jerusalem he was met by Jaddua the High Priest, whom he recognized from a dream and whom he thought was sent to him by divine intervention. Jaduaa is said to have read to him from the book of Daniel (8: 3-8, 20-22) which prophesized the Persian conquest. Whereas his original intent was to subjugate the Jews, his reign ended up being extraordinarily good for them. As long as his rule was acknowledged and accepted, the Jewish people had a remarkable degree of freedom and privilege.

Charles Seltman writes: "Alexander stands above all the great men of the past, supreme as soldier, ruler, organizer, as the clear thinker, the mystical dreamer who is also the intensely practical man of action; and he was equally brilliant as an economist. It is mainly this aspect of his personality that we can study through coinage."

The coinage of Alexander the Great was so extensive that his coins are still available today, twenty-four centuries later, at relatively reasonable prices. His coinage consisted of gold, silver, and copper and is significant for the new types he introduced, for the standards he based them on, and for the system of mints he established.

Tetradrachm, 325-323 B.C.

THE EARLY COINED MONEY
IN THE HOLY LAND

The standard gold coin was the stater with the head of the goddess Athena in a Corinthian helmet on the obverse, and a full figure of Nike, the winged goddess of victory, standing, holding a mast and a naval standard.

Drachm, 290-275 B.C.   **Stater, 280-260 B.C.**

He placed the head of Herakles, the greatest of all mythological heroes, on the obverse of his silver coins. Herakles is wearing a lion skin in recognition of being the legendary ancestor of the Macedonian kings. The reverse shows Zeus, the main god of the Greeks, seated, holding an eagle and sceptre. This was an appropriate coin for Alexander. It appealed both to Greeks and to those in the lands to be conquered, and it was representative of Alexander's heroism. In fact, many assume the idealized portrait of Herakles was actually Alexander himself. (In fact, it would be years after his death before there was a coin with his portrait.)

Both coins were struck according to the standards developed by Athens, not as homage to Athens but out of economic logic. Athens was the largest issuer of coins and this way Alexander could capitalize on the Athenian commercial reputation.

Alexander established a network of mints unlike anyone before him. It was a common procedure when a country was conquered to melt its old coins (but we know this didn't always happen, hence we have coins from other conquerors still circulating) and make new ones. There were twenty main mints in Europe, Asia Minor, Syria, Cyprus, Babylon, Alexandria, and of particular interest to us, Phoenicia and the Holy Land.

Four of the five cities in the area issued staters and tetradrachms. (The only major city that did not was Tyre because it was destroyed in battle.) Those that did were Aradus, Byblus, Sidon, and in the Holy Land itself, Akko. Many of the coins were struck using melted sigloi and darics, which perhaps helps explain that there are very few Persian coins found in Israeli archaeological excavations.

THE PTOLEMIES AND SELEUCIDS

Alexander's coinage was issued and circulated for many years after his death in 323 B.C., but his empire quickly faced civil war. His generals fought to divide the empire among themselves, and the area of the Holy Land moved back and forth between the Egyptian and Seleucid successors. Among the greatest of Alexander's generals was Ptolemy I Soter, to whom the Egyptian portion of the empire fell. He first attacked Jerusalem in 320 B.C. but it was not until 301 B.C. that the entire area came under Egyptian rule, forcing the Seleucids to retreat for a century.

THE EARLY COINED MONEY
IN THE HOLY LAND

Tetradrachm, Alexandria, 314-310 B.C.

Upon his accession, Ptolemy minted his own tetradrachms, which at first bore a striking resemblance to those of Alexander. The legend even read "an Alexander coin of Ptolemy," giving the king both authenticity and legitimacy. Before long, coins of a radically different design from Alexander's were introduced. The obverse featured the king himself with the breastplate of Zeus around his neck as a symbol of his divinity. The reverse was an eagle holding a thunderbolt. This became the basic Egyptian type for three centuries. Coins were minted at Akko, Ashkelon, Dora, and Gaza.

Tetradrachm, Alexandria, 285-272 B.C.

The Ptolemies ruled the Holy Land for about a century until a five-year old child, Ptolemy V, succeeded to the throne. This proved to be an opportune time for a Syrian resurgence, so the Seleucid king Antiochus III went on a campaign to restore some lost provinces, including the one in Palestine. In 201 B.C. he was readily welcomed into Jerusalem and until the end of his reign in 187 B.C., he made life better for the residents than it had been in some time. As we have already observed, this was a situation that would not last long. The reign of Antiochus IV (Epihanes) from 175-164 B.C. undid it all in the most tragic way possible.

Antiochus III The Great, King of Syria, 233-187 B.C.

The coins of the Seleucids in the Holy land were struck at the mints of Akko, Ashkelon, and Gaza in silver and bronze and were of a number of different types. The obverses usually show the head of the reigning monarch (Antiochus IV, VII, and VIII all struck coins there). The reverses varied from Zeus to Nike to a cornucopiae. The Hasmonean revolt that followed this reign had the side effect of introducing a whole new range of coins, native and exclusive to the Holy Land, which continued first with the acquiescence of the Seleucids and later as a colony under Rome.

Antiochus VIII Grypus,
King of Syria, 121-96 B.C.

THE COINAGE OF THE PHOENICIAN CITIES

Before looking at the Hasmonean coinage, we should look at another few series of coins connected to the Bible and with as much significance as any others, the coins of the trading cities of Phoenicia: Aradus, Sidon, and especially, Tyre. As the Seleucid Empire was being broken apart in the last 150 years B.C., these three cities took advantage of the chaos around them to establish and cement their freedom from external authority. Aradus was in many ways independent already and began issuing large amounts of silver tetradrachms starting c. 136 B.C. The largest portion of these had a veiled and turreted head of Tyche, the patron of the city and the goddess of fortune with a reverse showing Nike standing. Tyre achieved autonomy in 125 B.C. followed by Sidon in 111 B.C.

Tetradrachm of Aradus, 108 B.C.

The coinage of Sidon actually dates back to the end of the fifth century B.C. and the city probably claims most of the region's important coinage up to the time of Alexander the Great. We are concerned here with the coinage of its independence, primarily a large issue of tetradrachms that lasted until the advent of Roman rule. The obverse type is similar to that of Aradus, but the reverse has a Ptolemaic eagle standing on the prow of a galley.

Shekel of Sidon

The coinage of Tyre deserves special mention both for its volume and its significance. From 125 B.C. to about A.D. 70 it produced an enormous number of tetradrachms (or shekels) and half shekels with the laureate head of the city's great god, Melkart (Herakles) and the Ptolemaic eagle on a galley. For the entire time of its issue, its relative purity and weight remained consistent, making it the most important coin in the entire region.

THE EARLY COINED MONEY
IN THE HOLY LAND

One important way in which the Phoenician coins differed from their Seleucid predecessors is that they reverted from being based on the coins of Athens (the Attic standard) to a standard first instituted by the Ptolemies, which is now referred to as the "Phoenician standard." (A tetradrachm under the Attic standard weighed 17.5 grams, but 14.5 grams under the finer Phoenician one). This seemingly trivial statistic is in fact what makes these particular coins so important in the Bible.

It is an ancient Jewish tradition, with its roots harkening back to the sparing of the first born Hebrew sons from the tenth plague in Egypt, that the father of a first born son must redeem his new born with a payment of five shekels to a priest. The rabbis later specified that these shekels must be of "Tyrian weight." It is also known that because these coins had a silver content of over 90% they were considered to meet the biblical requirement that they be "pure," a stipulation that most other coins, with the exception of these Phoenician city issues and harder to find coins from Macedon, Thrace, Egypt, and Syria, did not satisfy.

These coins were also the coins used to pay the annual half shekel tax or tribute to the Temple in Jerusalem. Again, there was a stipulation that payments to the Temple must be in pure silver. Not only were these coins in plentiful supply, but also they were accepted readily by all who used them.

Numismatic historians Hendin and Meshorer point out that the shekels of Tyre were not only made in the city of Tyre, but also in Jerusalem! This happened in the first century A.D. when, although the production of Tyrian coins was due to be discontinued, they were still needed for religious obligations. Roman coins were not pure enough, so there is a theory that shekels of Tyre were minted in Jerusalem which, according to Meshorer, can distinguish them today by the mintmark "KP" to the right of the eagle.

Shekel, 159 B.C.

"Then one of the twelve, called Judas Iscariot, went unto the cheif priests, And said unto them, What will ye give me, and I will deliver him unto you? And they covenanted with him for thirty pieces of silver." (Matthew 26: 14-15)

THE THIRTY PIECES OF SILVER

There can hardly be doubt that the "thirty pieces of silver," said to have been received by Judas Iscariot in payment for his betrayal of Jesus, consisted of tetradrachms or shekels. Because the betrayal took place when and where it did, we can deduce the identity of the coins rather easily. The coins would have to have been coins circulating easily in Jerusalem at the time. The preponderance of evidence squarely falls first on the coin of Tyre, with the other Phoenician city coins, and some Ptolemaic and Seleucic coins possibly included. Since they all weighed the same and had the same value, any mix was possible.

Shekel, 10 B.C.

It is instructive that the most famous reference to the thirty pieces of silver is the last in the Bible. In fact, the number 30 has some historical relevance going as far back as Exodus (21: 32) where this was the amount that had to be paid to an owner on the account of the accidental death of a slave. Also, Zechariah (11: 12-13) mentions thirty shekels as the "price" of blood. Finally, in Matthew (28: 12,15), silver is referred to as being used to bribe the soldiers who had abandoned their watch to keep silent.

RHODES AND THE "JUDAS PENNIES"

The coinage of the Greek island of Rhodes provides an interesting insight into how misinformation can turn into legend. For about a century and a half, from circa 304 to 166 B.C., Rhodes' geographic location in the Aegean made it an independent maritime power with few equals.

Tetradrachm, 404-385 B.C.

Because the people on the island claimed to be descendants of the Sun god Helios, in tribute to him, they constructed a hundred foot tall statue and one of the wonders of the ancient world, the Colossus of Rhodes. Its distinctive head, with wind-blown hair and a crown of rays behind, was used as the model for the obverse of Rhodes' coins. This was relatively unique, as they substituted a full-face portrait for the profile view that was the standard. For the reverse, they chose Helios' emblem and the flower from which they got their name, a rose (rhodus in Greek).

This design remained fairly consistent from 400 B.C. until the victory by the Romans in 42 B.C., or nearly 400 years. Vast quantities of tetradrachms were produced, so many that during the Middle Ages, they were frequently unearthed by peasants in the course of their farming activities. Numismatist G.F. Hill informs us that some of these have been preserved in churches under the name "Judas Pennies," as vestiges of Christ's betrayal. Why? The medieval clerics thought that the sun god Helios was actually Christ wearing his crown of thorns and the rose of Rhodes was really the Rose of Jericho and symbolic of the Resurrection.

JEWISH COINAGE

JEWISH COINAGE

Among the privileges Antiochus VII granted Simon in 139 B.C. included the "... leave also to coin money for thine own country with thine own stamp." Nonetheless, it seems clear today that he never did so, and in any case, Sidetes later revoked the right. The coins once attributed to this Simon actually belonged to Simon Bar-Kochba. We know this because close study revealed that these coins bearing the name "Simon" were struck on other Roman and Greek coins which did not exist during the time of Simon Maccabee. In addition, the style of some of the lettering on the coins is out of character for the early date. The responsibility of striking the first "exclusively Jewish" coins fell to Simon's successors.

Until now we have been discussing coins exclusively made of precious metal. Logic and not a degree in economics should be sufficient for anyone to realize that these coins would not have been necessary, or even within the affordability of your typical "everyman" for use in daily commerce. We know, for instance, that a loaf of bread cost approximately one eighth of a drachm, which would have been an average day's salary. A money of account, that is, coinage for common usage, was also needed and that is where coins of bronze play a role. Many small Seleucid bronzes stayed in circulation for hundreds of years, and they were complemented by the Judean coins that followed them.

Designs on Jewish Coins

We have seen how all their neighbors came to highlight the images of gods, people, and animals on their many coin issues. For the Jews, this presented a problem. A strict interpretation of the numerous prohibitions against idolatry in scripture precluded the depiction of "graven images" and thus any human or animal form on coins. There was also a later Talmudic restriction on the depiction of items used in the Holy Temple, such as the seven-branched candelabrum (menorah), and other sacred objects such as certain musical instruments. There was even a prohibition on an accurate rendition of the Temple structure itself

Encumbered by these restrictions, the Jews turned to a whole array of symbols instead. We owe their categorization to the 1944 study of them by Dr. Paul Romanoff of the Museum of the Jewish Theological Seminary of America. Romanoff puts them in five categories: agricultural, buildings, astronomical, utensils, and symbols.

Agricultural symbols form the largest category and consist of the following:

Palm tree: This is a carry over from numerous Greek coins, particularly from the islands in the Mediterranean. It also appears on some Palestinian coins. There appears to be no religious significance and it was probably used as an example of native flora and for geographic symbolism.

Palm branch: A symbol of victory and honor on non-Jewish coins. Here it could also be symbolic of ritual.

Lulav: A group of palm, myrtle, and willow branches bound together and used in the Feast of Tabernacles (Sukkot) festival ritual.

Etrog: A citron used in conjunction with the lulav above.

Vine and/or grapes: Important in commerce and of special significance in many Jewish rituals. They denote blessing and the fertility of the land and are also said to symbolic of Jerusalem, the Torah and the patriarchs.

Pomegranate: Usually portrayed as three fruits on a single stem, it was one of the most famous products of the Holy Land. It was used as part of the High Priest's wardrobe and represented a host of attributes: blessing, fertility, piety, good works, and wisdom.

Lily: Used prodigiously in Temple decoration, it was considered the finest of flora. It evolved into the flower symbol of Israel. On the Jewish coins it bears a strong resemblance to a rose, giving rise to speculation that this style was chosen to capitalize on the recognition enjoyed by the coins of Rhodes.

Cornucopiae: The horn of plenty was a symbol used on many coins of the ancients and was universally recognized and understood. It is thought that it was placed on coins to assist in trade.

 Wreath: Wreaths were used in celebrations and were symbolic of leadership and power. They serve to ennoble whatever they surround. Meshorer, the late Israeli numismatic scholar, tells us that the manner in which wreaths sometimes surround the name of the ruler is symbolic of the wreath on the head of ruler on traditional coins.

There are five types showing what Romanoff called "utensils." All of them have a connection to ritual:

The Bar Kokhba War, A.D. 132-135
Large Bronze

1. The amphora was the common way for the ancients to ship and store liquids, including the water, wine, and oil used in the Temple. It is possible that as the Menorah was considered too holy to be put on coins, the amphora was used instead because one of its functions was to hold the oil that fed the Menorah's lamps.

The Bar Kokhba War, A.D. 133/134
Denarius

2. The ampula was a narrow-necked, one-handled jug used in the Temple in the water-libation ritual of the Sukkot festival. It was a prayer for rain during the coming growing season. After the Temple's destruction, the ritual could not be performed, and we can speculate that the appearance of this device on a coin was intended as a substitute and remembrance that could have the same effect.

The Jewish War, A.D. 66-70
Shekel

3. The omer-cup or chalice was not meant for liquids but was a golden utensil used in the first grain harvest, known as the omer. On the second day of Passover, when the first reapings of the harvest were coming in, an offering of barley was given the Temple. It was placed in the omer-cup and was hoped to have the effect of suspending the rains during the harvest.

The Bar Kokhba War, A.D. 132-135
Denarius or Zuz, Year 2 (133/134)

4. Trumpets had a specific function in the Temple when they were blown during sacrifices, the Sukkot water-libation ceremony, on fast days, and in special prayers for rain. Since these only appeared on coins after the Temple's destruction, we can assume the same motive as for the ampula above.

The Bar Kokhba War, A.D. 132-135
Denarius, A.D.133/134

5. Lyres and harps also are shown on only the latest coins. Their use in the Temple was celebratory, and they are symbolic of the prayers in the Temple that were recited to the accompaniment of music. Their appearance on coins implies that they would be used again on the occasion of the Temple's reconstruction.

In the category of buildings, the only structure used is the Temple, and it only appears at the very end of the series of Jewish coinage, with those of Bar-Kochba. It is possible that the intent was to portend the reconstruction of the destroyed Holy Temple. There is debate about the style of the temple shown, which is considered "schematic." Perhaps this was to circumvent the prohibition against depicting the Temple, or perhaps it was a part of its facade or interior. No one actually knows.

The Hasmoneans,
Alexander Jannaeus, A.D. 103-76

The Hasmoneans,
Alexander Jannaeus, A.D. 103-76

The astronomical category comprises the Menorah and a star. The Menorah symbolized the planets and was situated in such a way in the Temple as to conform to some particular religious and astrological ideas. It was prohibited to depict the Temple's Menorah and it appears on only one rare and exceptional coin of Matthias Antigonus, which we will discuss shortly. The star is probably suggestive of the morning star (Venus), the sun, or the heavens. Another important symbol is the anchor. It was originally a Seleucid symbol referring to that empire's naval power.

THE VALUE OF A MITE

The smallest and most common coin in ancient Israel and certainly the most common coin in the life of Jesus was the bronze lepton. In English, non-collectors may be more familiar with the term mite, which is an appropriate moniker for something so incredibly tiny. Lepton, however, is the proper term and in Greek means "small" or "thin." It was also called a half prutah and was one of a number of bronze coins produced by the Jews. There was also the prutah, another very small coin and the 1/6 shekel. According to Hendin, the lepton was the equivalent of 384 drachmae. In other words, in took nearly four hundred of these small poins to have the same spending power as one silver coin. Imagine needing four hundred U.S. cents to make up one dollar! Hendin also tells us it took forty-eight lepta to buy a loaf of bread. One amazing thing about these lepta was that they circulated for hundreds of years, a fact that is confirmed by the presence of the early ones in coin finds with issues from a century and more later.

THE WIDOW'S MITE

"And Jesus sat over against the treasury, and beheld how the people cast money into the treasury: and many that were rich cast in much. And there came a certain poor widow, and she threw in two mites, which make a farthing. And he called unto him his disciples, and saith unto them, Verily I say unto you, That this poor widow hath cast more in, than all they which have cast into the treasury. For all they did cast in of their abundance; but she of her want did cast in all that she had, even all her living" (Mark 12: 41-44)

"And he looked up and saw the rich men casting their gifts into the treasury. And he saw also a certain poor widow casting in thither two mites. And he said, Of a truth I say unto you, that this poor widow hath cast in more than they all" (Luke 21: 1-3)

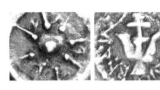

Widow's Mites

The story of the Widow's Mite is one of the most famous biblical passages pertaining to coins. Considering that she was destitute, the widow could only have given two lepta to the Temple. Although the event took place during the reign of Herod Antipas, we can be fairly certain, owing to the scarcity of these coins today, that the Antipas issues were not the coins used. Then and now, the most common of all the lepta are those of Alexander Jannaeus, and it is more than likely that these are the coins. Although they date to an earlier generation (103-76 B.C.), there is no doubt that they were as prevalent then as they are now. In fact, you can still buy a lepton of Alexander Jannaeus for less than you will spend on many common American silver dollars.

THE MONEYCHANGERS

"And Jesus went into the Temple of God, and cast out all them that sold and bought in the temple, and overthrew the tables of the moneychangers and the seats of them that sold doves, And I said unto them, It is written my house shall be called the house of prayer, but ye have made it into a den of thieves" (Matthew 21:12-13)

This episode took place at Passover, when Jerusalem was mobbed with pilgrims celebrating the festival. All who came had to make a cash donation to the Temple, but what coins could they use? They came from different places where different currencies circulated. If the pilgrims did not have a coin conforming to the specification for the Temple tribute money, they had to exchange the money they had for a type (probably a local copper issue) that was acceptable Jewish coin. As in any airport or bank today, the moneychangers did this for a fee (generally eight percent). They were able to set their own rates, but some of them did not personify the most impeccable ethical standards, and their business practices reflected it. Furthermore, the moneychangers set their operations up adjacent to the Temple gates, and would compete with each other for the best location possible. This is the kind of conduct that so infuriated Jesus.

HASMONEAN COINAGE

Hasmonean Coinage

John Hyrcanus I (135-104 B.C.)

    John Hyrcanus I

It is interesting that the first coin resembling the Hasmonean style was actually a Seleucid issue of King Antiochus VII Sidetes (138-129 B.C.) struck at Jerusalem. This is the same king who gave Simon Maccabe the right to strike coins, a right he never exercised. Since Simon was murdered in 134 B.C. and Antiochus died in 129 B.C., this coin must have been made between those two dates. The obverse shows a lily, which on a full-struck specimen would be within a border of dots. The reverse shows an anchor, often described as upside down (It is not. When an anchor was not in the water it was kept in an inverted position so it could be more readily thrown into the water when needed. It is only upside down to a fish!). The Greek legend has the name of King Antiochus and the dates of the Seleucid era of or which correspond to regnal years 181 and 182 (approximately 132-131 B.C.).

It is likely that Antiochus issued this coin to mark his success in Jerusalem in 133 B.C. As he developed his alliance of necessity with Simon's son John Hyrcanus, it is possible that this coin was one of the results.

In reality, the Hasmonean alliance with the Seleucids made them a client state. It also made it possible for Hyrcanus to strike his own coins and he began a series, which continued virtually without interruption until the Hasmonean family was ousted by the Romans. There are a large number of prutahs and lepta in existence and with one very rare exception (a double prutah with a helmet on one side and a double cornucopia on the other), they all have the same basic design. The obverse is always a lengthy Hebrew legend of four to five lines enclosed within a wreath, translating as Yehohanan High Priest and Head of the Council of the Jews (probably meaning the Sanhedrin). The reverse shows a pomegranate between two cornucopiae, probably in imitation of the coins of Syria.

Judah Aristobulus (104-103 B.C.)

    Judah Aristobulus

52

John's eldest took the title of king soon after sending his mother and her husband's designated heir to prison and having her starved to death. His reign of not much more than a year was marked by war and palace intrigue. The few (and quite rare) prutah coins he struck are similar to his predecessor's but with a legend that reads Yehuda the High Priest and Head of the Council of the Jews.

Alexander Jannaeus (103-76 B.C.)

Alexander Jannaeus

Alexander Jannaeus

After the death of Aristobulus, the eldest of his three remaining brothers took over and dispatched his siblings, one to death and the other to private life. His long reign was marked first by wars of conquest and later by internal conflict. Only towards the end of his life did he find himself on better terms with most of the populace, in particular the Pharisees.

The coinage of Alexander Jannaeus, both prutahs and lepta, was so prodigious that they are cheap even today. They are noteworthy for a number of different types and legends in Hebrew, Greek, and Aramaic. It has been suggested that the diversity in language was for the benefit of those who did not speak Hebrew (in actuality, the lingua franca of the time was Aramaic). When he took over, he continued to issue the traditional bronze coins with the Hebrew legend reading Yehonatan the High Priest and Head of the Council of the Jews on one side and the double cornucopiae on the other.

There was also number of other types that had the legend Yehonatan the King on each side, but Hebrew on one and Greek on the other. They are:

1. Obverse: a half-opened lily. Reverse: anchor.

2. Obverse: palm branch. Reverse: flower.

3. Obverse: star. Reverse: anchor.
(Note: There is one variety of this type in which the text says King Alexandros Year 25 in Greek and Aramaic.)

John Hyrcanus II (67, 63-40 B.C.)

 John Hyrcanus II

Modern research has shown that Alexander's wife and successor, Salome Alexandra, issued no coins. We have already discussed the dispute between her sons when she died. Aristobulus II struck no coins. It seems evident that those of Hyrcanus II came after he was reestablished by Pompey after the Roman intervention. The legends on these prutahs reverts to the earlier type and, as a result of Pompey's edict, omits any reference to "king." Yonatan the High Priest and Head of the Council of the Jews. The designs also revert to the early Hasmonean style of legends and double cornucopiae.

Mattathias Antigonus (40-37 B.C.)

The last Hasmonean coinage includes the most unusual. It is important to realize that by this time there were in essence two rulers: Antigonus with the support of the short-lived Parthian invasion and Herod I under the aegis of Rome. Perhaps to make a statement of authority, as Meshorer suggests, the coins of Antigonus are by far the largest, the most impressive, and exist in more denominations than those of any of his predecessors. In addition to prutahs, coins were also made on much larger flans. They can be broken down into three groups:

Large: these are from .9 to one inch in diameter. The obverse shows a double cornucopiae with the legend Mattatayah the High Priest and Head of the Council of the Jews. There is an ivy wreath on the reverse and the Greek legend King Antoionus. He did not have the Seleucids to concern him any longer, hence the title.

 **Large**
Mattathias Antigonus,
Mattatayah, 40-37 B.C.

Medium: these range from .75 to .85 inches. The obverse has a cornucopia tied with a ribbon and sometimes with a bunch of grapes hanging over it. The legend is reduced to Mattatayah the High Priest. King Antigonus is the legend on the other side in two, three or four lines found within a wreath and a border of dots. (91-235)

Medium
Mattathias Antigonus,
Mattatayah, 40-37 B.C.

Prutahs: these are larger than seen previously, as they are slightly more than 1/2 inch in diameter. There are several types. Two of them have the legend as on the large coins and either a single or double cornucopiae. The third is one of the rarest and most famous of all Jewish coins. It is a prutah of about .55 inch dimension. On one side it has the seven-branched Menorah from the Holy Temple. The reverse has what was described in one nineteenth-century source as "an object represented by a horizontal line from which rise four verticals," and another said it was "four parallel trees." In 1914, another source called it a "tetrastyle screen between the Holy Place and the Holy of Holies." It is generally recognized today to be the "showbread table" from the Temple. (Showbread, or shewbread means "presence bread." They were twelve loaves of unleavened bread placed by the priests in the Temple on the Sabbath, which were to be eaten by them alone at the end of the week.) Both these objects were among those of which reproduction was expressly forbidden. The two items were placed opposite each other in the Holy of Holies and were its two most sacred items. Meshorer speculates that Antigonus took the drastic step of putting these items on his coins in a last ditch effort to spur the people to protect their sacred objects in the face of the assault by the pagan Herod. If so, that would date this coin to 37 B.C., making it the last Hashmonean coin.

Prutah, Jerusalem, 37 B.C.

THE COINS OF THE
HERODIAN DYNASTY

The Coins of the Herodian Dynasty

Herod the Great (40-4 B.C.)

Herod's coins clearly illustrate his Hellenistic world view. None of his coins have any Hebrew inscriptions on them, usually only the name King Herod in Greek. He was careful, however, not to overdo the offense to the populace, so the devices used on the coins largely avoided graven images, but still showed something of a Greco-Roman slant. Only bronze coins were made, as Pompey strictly forbade the coinage of silver in most of the region's mints. (even though shekels of Tyre were minted in Jerusalem at about this time.) Most of the coins were prutahs, with a few lepta, and one series with larger denominations of two, four and eight prutahs.

Herod I, The Great, 40-38/7 B.C.
2 Prutot

Herod I, The Great, 40-4 B.C.
4 Prutot

Herod I, The Great, 40-38/7 B.C.
8 Prutot

The largest two coins both show a helmet with cheek pieces on one side. The other side of the 8-prutah is a tripod with a bowl on top. These are obviously Roman symbols, which were used in religious rituals. The 4-prutah has a decorated military shield on its reverse, in all likelihood as a paean to the Roman army. The 2-prutah shows a winged caduceus with a poppy flower on the reverse. The caduceus was the symbol of the god Mercury, and the poppy was a symbol of the cult of the goddess Demeter.

There was a variety of one-prutah coins with the basic types as follows:

1) Obverse: an acrostolium (a nautical instrument for measuring wind speed). Reverse: palm branch

      Herod I, The Great

2) Obverse: a tripod table. Reverse: a diadem (ornamental headband), sometimes with a cross in center, sometimes not, but regardless, not concerning Christianity.

Herod I, The Great

3) Obverse: tripod table. Reverse: branch of palm or vine

4) Obverse: anchor. Reverse: inscription.

Herod I, The Great, 40-38/7 B.C.
Prutah

5) Obverse: anchor. Reverse: double cornucopia.

There were also two issues of lepton:

1) Obverse: cornucopia. Reverse: eagle.
This seems to be the first graven image on a coin. It is said to represent the gold eagle Herod erected at the gate of his Temple.

Herod I, The Great

2) Obverse: anchor. Reverse: galley.
This coin is said to honor the opening of the harbor at Caesarea.

Herod I, The Great

Herod Archelaus (4 B.C. - A.D. 6)

Archelaus did not assume the title of "king," so his coins say or abbreviate "Ethnarch" in Greek. Nearly all of his coins have a nautical theme. There are 2 and 1-prutot with a double cornucopiae on one side and a war galley on the other. Other prutah coins with this subject include:

1) Obverse: anchor. Reverse: double cornucopiae or inscription.

Herod Archelaus

2) Obverse: prow of galley. Reverse: inscription

Herod Archelaus

There is also a prutah with a military helmet on one side and a vine branch and grapes on the other.

Herod Antipas (4 B.C. - A.D. 39)

The Herod of the Gospels, his coins were generally of one basic design: a palm branch on the obverse and a Greek inscription within a wreath, usually a variation of Herod Tetrarch, on the other. On a few coins, the inscription is the name of the city of Tiberius, meant to commemorate its founding.

Herod Antipas, 4 B.C. - A.D. 39
Eighth Denomination,
Tiberias, Year 24 (A.D. 20/1)

Herod Antipas, 4 B.C. - A.D. 39
Full Denomination,
Tiberias, Year 43 (A.D. 39/40)

60

THE COINS OF THE HERODIAN DYNASTY

Herod Antipas

Many of Herod Antipas' coins are dated with Greek letters indicating the year of his reign. All of the coins of this reign are quite scarce. Despite its length, coins were only made in five years: 24, 33, 34, 37 and 43, corresponding roughly to A.D. 19-39 There were four denominations, which followed the Roman standard. The largest bronze coins were made the equivalent of 1/8 of a denarius and the others,1/16, 1/32, and 1/64, respectively. They are also commonly called "Full, Half, Quarter, and Eighth Denominations."

Herod Antipas, 4 B.C. - A.D. 39
Half Denomination,
Tiberias, Year 43 (A.D. 39/40)

Herod Antipas, 4 B.C. - A.D. 39
Quarter Denomination,
Tiberias, Year 43 (A.D. 39/40)

Herod Philip (4 B.C. - A.D. 34)

Under Philip we see a radical departure, in that we find human images, in the form of the heads of Augustus, Tiberius, and Livia on the coins. It is probable that he was able to do this because the area of his tetrarchy was far removed and there were very few Jewish residents. So it is possible that this could have actually been more in keeping with local mores. One coin exists with the head of Philip and a reverse of the head of Augustus, but most others show a temple with four columns, which is the temple built by his father in Paneas in 10 B.C. Most of these coins ranged in size from a half to an inch in diameter similar to those above.

Philip, 4 B.C. - A.D. 34
Caesarea Paneas, Year 5 (A.D.1/2)

Philip, 4 B.C. - A.D. 34
Caesarea Paneas,
Year 33 (A.D. 29/30)

Herod Agrippa I (37-43 A.D.)

Herod the Great's grandson was educated in Rome and made that apparent on his coins. There is only one distinctively Jewish type, a prutah with a canopy resembling an umbrella on the obverse and three ears of barley on the reverse. The canopy was a symbol of royalty and represents Agrippa's kingly status. The barley is symbolic of the land of plenty. There have been many of this issue found in Jerusalem, and it has been suggested that this coin was made specifically for use by the Jews.

Philip, 4 B.C. - A. D. 34
Prutah, Jerusalem, Year 6 (A.D. 41/42)

All other coins of Agrippa I are "profane" types depicting the Emperor Tiberius, Agrippa himself, his son, and his brother. The reverses are typical Roman colonial types, including temples and goddesses. There is one very rare coin showing clasped hands as a symbol of the friendship between Agrippa and the Emperor.

Agrippa I, A.D. 37-44
Caesarea Paneas, Year 2 (A.D. 37/8)
Medium Bronze

62

There are also some very rare coins of Roman colonial type from another Herod, Agrippa's brother, Herod of Chalcis. He was a close friend of Emperor Claudius and was given the Syrian state of Chalcis. He was also given authority from afar over the Temple. Chalcis was given to Agrippa II when he died.

***Herod, Brother of Agrippa I
and King of Chalcis, A.D. 41-48
Chalcis, Year 3 (A.D. 43/4)***

Herod Agrippa II (A.D. 50-100)

The last ruler of Herod's dynasty also had the longest and most extensive coinage. In it were denominations such as the assarion and its multiples and fractions, which were struck in four mints. He also had two series of coins that were dated differently (one was based on the year A.D. 56 when he received the title of king; the other is reckoned from A.D. 61 when he established the city of Neronias.) His rule spanned the lives of the emperors Nero, Galba, Otho, Vitellius, Vespasian, Titus, Domitian, Nerva, and Trajan.

***Agrippa II,
A.D. 50-100***

In many ways, Agrippa II's issues were really nothing more than regular Roman colonial coins with the bust of the emperor and typical reverses. They would sometimes refer to Agrippa by name, but more often not. Overall, they are indicative of what had become the Herodian dynasty's total subservience to Rome.

COINS OF THE ROMAN
PROCURATORS OF JUDEA

Coins of the Roman Procurators of Judea

As we have already seen, except for a short break within the Herodian period, Judea was actually governed by Rome's prefects and procurators from A.D. 6 to 66. The coinage of the procurators is unique in Roman coinage annals in that it breaks from the Roman standards of style and design and is mostly "Jewish" in character, at least up to the time of Pontius Pilate. All the coins were of the prutah denomination and were minted in enormous quantities. The names of the procurators are never mentioned on the coins, but we know who they are because the inscriptions date the coins by the regnal year of the Roman emperor. The inscriptions were in Greek so the local inhabitants could understand the coins.

Of the fourteen procurators from A.D. 6 to 66, only six of them issued coins, as follows:

Under Emperor Augustus (27 B.C. - A.D. 14):

Coponius, 1st procurator, (A.D. 6-9)

  Lepton of Coponius

An ear of corn or barley is on the obverse of this issue while the reverse shows a palm tree from which hang bunches of dates. The Greek letters in the field indicate the coin is from the 36th year of the reign of Augustus.

Marcus Ambibulus, 2nd procurator (A.D. 9-12)
The design is the same as preceding with regnal years 39, 40, or 41.

Under Emperor Tiberius (A.D. 14-37):

Valerius Gratus. 4th procurator (A.D. 15-25)

  Valerius Gratus, A.D. 15-16

  Valerius Gratus, A.D. 16-17

COINS OF THE ROMAN
PROCURATORS OF JUDEA

Valerius Gratus, A.D. 17-18

Valerius Gratus, A.D. 18-19

Gratus was procurator for eleven years and in that time made a number of different coins types, starting with regal year 2 of Tiberius.

1) Obverse: inscription Cae-sar in wreath. Reverse: double cornucopia. Regnal year 2.

2) Obverse: inscription Jul-ia (mother of Tiberius) in wreath. Reverse: palm branch. Regnal year 2.

3) Obverse: as above. Reverse: double cornucopia. Regnal year 3.

4) Obverse: as above. Reverse: a triple lily. Regnal year 3.

Valerius Gratus

5) Obverse: vine branch with leaf and bunch of grapes, Julia. Reverse: thin-necked amphora with two handles. Regnal year 4.

6) Obverse: vine branch with leaf and bunch of grapes, Tiberius. Reverse: thick-necked kantharos with two handles. Regnal year 4.

Valerius Gratus

7) Obverse: name of Tiberius in wreath. Reverse: palm branch. Regnal years 4, 5, and 11.

Valerius Gratus

Pontius Pilate, 5th procurator (A.D. 26-36)

Pontius Pilate, Year 16

Pontius Pilate, Year 16

We have already discussed Pilate in sufficient detail to understand how his coins would have appeared offensive to the Jews. It has been pointed out that if he had really wanted to offend them he would have placed the bust of the emperor on the coin. Regardless, the use of Roman priestly implements was a radical and insensitive move. There were only two coins types made and in only three different years.

The first is from year 16 of Tiberius and has a simpulum (a form of ladle) with the name of the emperor and the year. The reverse shows three ears of barley below Julia's name and title. The second type is from years 16, 17, and 18. The obverse has a lituus (a curved wand used by Roman priests) surrounded by the name and title of Tiberius. The reverse bears the date in a wreath.

Under Claudius (A.D. 41-54):

Antoninus Felix, the 11th procurator (A.D. 52-59)

Antonius Felix, Under Claudius

The procurators returned to Judea after death of Agrippa I and two of the final seven issued coins. All of the coins of Antoninus Felix were made in A.D. 54, the 14th and last year of Emperor Claudius. Although the number of types were few, the quantity was many and these, too, are readily available today.

The first type has an obverse with two crossed palm branches and Claudius' name and title around them along with the date in the field. On the reverse is the name Julia Agrippina, wife of Claudius, in a wreath.

The other type is one of the most interesting of the procuratorial types. On the obverse, copied from Roman coins, are two crossed shields and spears, a reference to Roman power. They have the names of Claudius' two sons, Nero Claudius on the obverse and Britannicus (BRIT) on the reverse, which also has a palm tree and the regnal year.

Antonius Felix, Under Claudius

Porcius Festus, 12th procurator (A.D. 59-62)

Quandrans of Porcius Festus

Quandrans of Porcius Festus

The last coin of the procurators again assumes a Jewish identity. They all have the familiar palm branch obverse and a reverse with an inscription of Nero's name in a wreath. The regnal year 5 is on the obverse, but so many of these coins have been found that it is possible that they were struck in later years, as well.

COINS OF THE FIRST REVOLT
AND SECOND REVOLT

Coins of the First Revolt (The Jewish War) A.D. 66-70

A procurator who did not issue coins, Gessius Florus, the fourteenth and last, is nonetheless responsible for one of the most famous and important series of coins in all of numismatics, the silver shekels and half shekels of the Jewish War. Florus could arguably have given Pilate a run for his money in the category of "most reviled." At least Pilate did not spark an armed revolution. Florus' oppressions were of such magnitude that in A.D. 66, previously disputatious factions of Jews united long enough to chase the Romans from Jerusalem.

One of the first things the Jews did was assume the emperor's right of silver coinage. They chose to create a coin, a silver shekel, unique to the people of Israel, steeped in their own symbols and traditions, without naming any one individual as their leader. In fact, we do not know who actually issued them. The legend of the obverse of the coin is simple and direct: shekel of Israel. This is one of the very few ancient coins, Meshorer reminds us, to bear a denomination. After all, coins in those days were valued based on their size and weight. In other words, this was a statement of independence; no longer would shekels of Tyre be required for Temple payments. They were now obsolete.

The device chosen for the obverse was the golden omer-cup used in the Temple during the harvest festival on the second day of Passover:

"... When ye be come into the land which I give unto you, and shall reap the harvest thereof, then ye shall bring a sheaf of the first fruits of your harvest unto the priest: And he shall wave the sheaf before the Lord, to be accepted for you." (Leviticus 23: 10-11)

The reverse inscription, Jerusalem the Holy, is reminiscent of the legend on Tyre's coins: *"Of Tyre, Holy and Inviolate."* The design shows three pomegranates as they are about to turn from flower to fruit. Although we do not give the pomegranate much attention today, it was extraordinarily important to Jews as a symbol of fertility and abundance.

Besides shekels, half and quarter shekels were also struck, with the half shekel perhaps especially important as this was the value required for the Temple tax. The quarter shekel was equal in value to the denarius, Rome's standard silver coin. Few were made and today they are of the highest rarity.

Jewish War, A.D. 66-70
Half Shekel, Jerusalem, Year 2 (A.D. 67/68)

COINS OF THE FIRST REVOLT
(THE JEWISH WAR) A.D. 66-70

All the shekels, halves, and quarters have dates ranging from Year 1 to Year 5. Titus struck the shekel of Year 5 during the last four months of the siege of Jerusalem. Few survive today as most were probably seized by the Romans and melted.

Jewish War, A.D. 66-70
Shekel, Jerusalem, Year 5

Coins in bronze were also issued commencing in Year 2. In that year, they were all of the prutah denomination and in style are evocative of some earlier Jewish coins. The obverse has a two-handled amphora and Year 2 with a vine branch and leaf on the reverse along with the inscription "Freedom of Zion." Huge quantities of these were minted; whether for political or economic reason is anyone's guess, but the answer is probably both. Although its actual value is not certain, best estimates are that it was the equivalent of the Roman quadrans and that it took 64 of them to make a denarius and 256 for a shekel.

Jewish War, A.D. 66-70
Prutah, Jerusalem, Year 2
(A.D. 67/68)

Bronze prutot were made in the second and third years of the revolt (A.D. 67-68). In both these years, too, the coins had an amphora on the obverse and a vine leaf on the reverse. Meshorer points out that from here forward the vine leaf was one of the main Jewish decorative symbols.

COINS OF THE FIRST REVOLT
(THE JEWISH WAR) A.D. 66-70

By the fourth year, as things were taking a turn for the worse, the coinage changed dramatically from silver to gold. Silver must have been in short supply and those silver coins that were struck would have been with respect to the requirements of the Temple tax. Bronze coins of the same denominations were struck for public use. Thus we now find bronze eighth and quarter half shekels issued as emergency money. The devices on these coins are connected to the Feast of Tabernacles (Sukkot) and have the legend changed from "Freedom of Zion" to "Redemption of Zion." The half shekel has an etrog between two lulavs on one side and a palm tree between baskets of fruit on the other; the quarter shekel has an etrog on one side and two lulavs on the other; the eighth shekel has a lulav between two etrogs backed up by an omer cup.

Jewish War, A.D. 66-70
Large Half, Jerusalem, Year 4 (A.D. 69/70)

Jewish War, A.D. 66-70
Medium Quarter, Jerusalem, Year 4 (A.D. 69/70)

Jewish War, A.D. 66-70
Small Eighth, Jerusalem, Year 4 (A.D. 69/70)

Since Sukkot was a holiday celebrated in the Temple, which drew many pilgrims, it is possible that the coins were meant to evoke the ritual. These coins are also the first upon which the Jews used a palm tree, perhaps because the palm tree was also known as the "tree of life."

Coins of the Second Revolt (the Bar-Kochba War) A.D. 132-135

Just three and a half years in duration, the Second Revolt is nonetheless responsible for an extraordinary number of coin varieties. Knowledge about the revolt is of relatively recent vintage as a result of archaeological finds from the 1960s. One of the most interesting aspects of the coinage is, as we found in the discussion of Simon Maccabee, that the coins were not struck on fresh metal blanks but were instead overstruck on coins removed from circulation. In particular, those of the Emperors Trajan are quite commonly seen, but also encountered are many from as far back as Nero up to those of Nerva. There were also some from the contemporary ruler, Hadrian. Various Greek drachms and tetradrachms were also used.

A simple filing process was all that was needed for the bronze pieces. The image was removed, smoothing the surface in the process. All that was then needed was the new strike. It was not so simple for the silver pieces as excessive filing would have removed too much silver and diminished a coin's weight and thus its value. Therefore, a two-step process was developed. First, the retrieved coins were smashed with hammers to flatten them. Next the rims were adjusted from the damage done by the hammering, and they were then pounded back into shape suitable for striking.

The silver coins were of two sizes: the tetradrachm and the quarter tetradrachm (i.e., drachma or denarius). The source for the larger issue, which is now referred to as selas rather than shekels, came predominantly from Roman colonial silver tetradrachms struck at the mints of Antioch and Tyre. The small coins for the most part were overstruck on Roman imperial denarii and went by the name of zuz (plural zuzim).

As is common with all ancient bronze coins, the bronze issues of the Second Revolt are categorized by their size. There were any number of different coins circulating as "money of account" and all of it was used for overstiking. They were broken down into "large," "medium," and "small" bronzes. A medium bronze measured about one inch in diameter.

Allowing for stylistic differences, the silver selas maintained the same design throughout their time of issue. The obverse is a "schematic" facade of the Temple destroyed six decades earlier. It is made up of four pillars on a base. Between the middle pillars is a representation of the Ark of the Covenant.

The Bar Kokhba War,
A.D. 132-135
Tetradrachm or
Sela, Year 2
(A.D. 133/134)

There is a debate among scholars whether this is the Temple as it was or as Bar-Kochba would want it to be when he rebuilt it. Either way, the symbolism portends the future of Jerusalem and the Temple as the central locale in Judaism. It is also apparent that this "rough" image was used to avoid violating the injunction against accurately portraying the Temple or its ritual objects. The reverse takes the same theme as the coins of the First Revolt, the lulav with the etrog now placed to the left of it in accordance with the ordained Hebrew ritual.

The coins of the first year are dated Year one of the redemption of Israel. In the second year, redemption is replaced by freedom. Later issues bear no year but mention Jerusalem's redemption.

The zuzim or denarii exist with only two obverse types for the duration of their issue. One is a cluster of grapes with a branch and leaf; the other an olive wreath with tendrils surrounding a legend.

There are a number of reverse types, all of which are related to the Temple service and which are paired in various combinations with the two obverses. They are:

1) The golden flagon next to a palm branch.

The Bar Kokhba War, A.D. 132-135
Denarius or Zuz, Year 2 (A.D. 133/134)

2) A large palm branch.

The Bar Kokhba War, A.D. 132-135
Denarius or Zuz, Hybrid Issue of Years 1 and 2
A.D. 133/134

3) *A pair of upright trumpets.*

The Bar Kokhba War, A.D. 132-135
Denarius or Zuz, Year 2 (A.D. 133/134)

4) *A wide or narrow lyre.*

The Bar Kokhba War, A.D. 132-135
Denarius or Zuz, Year 2 (A.D. 133/134)

COINS OF THE SECOND REVOLT
(THE BAR-KOCHBA WAR) A.D. 132-135

The bronze coinage of the Bar-Kochba War is limited to just a few types. The very elusive large bronzes were struck in all three years and occur in only one type. Obverse: An inscription within a wreath (Simon or Jerusalem). Reverse: An amphora with two handles and the date.

The Bar Kokhba War, A.D. 132-135
Denarius or Zuz, Year 2 (A.D. 133/134)

There are two types of medium bronzes. One has a seven-branched palm tree with two clusters of dates on the obverse, with a reverse of a large vine leaf. The second shows an upright palm branch within a wreath on the front and a lyre on the reverse.

The Bar Kokhba War, A.D. 132-135
Medium, Year 1 (A.D. 132/133)

The Bar Kokhba War, A.D. 132-135
Medium, Year 1 (A.D. 132/133)

There is only one type of small bronze, showing a bunch of grapes hanging from a twig on the obverse and a palm tree reverse.

The Bar Kokhba War, A.D. 132-135
Small, Year 1 (A.D. 132/133)

The legends are similar on all the above coins. The obverse usually has a name, either Shimon, Jerusalem, or in the first year, Eleazar the Priest. The reverse had the dating conventions described above for years one, two and later.

So ends the ancient coinage of the Jews. Roman imperial policy allowed cities to establish mints and strike coins for their local needs, but these issues reflected the mores of a mixed and often heathen population. They were typical "Roman" colonial coins in every respect. The next "Jewish" coin minted in the Holy Land would be in 1948.

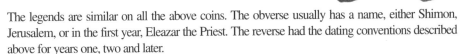

ROMAN COINS AND THE HOLY LAND

ROMAN COINS AND THE HOLY LAND

"Provide neither gold, nor silver, nor brass in your purses" (Matthew 10: 9).

Other than this very general reference, no gold coin is specifically mentioned in the New Testament. Up to four other Roman coins are: the as, the dupondius, and the quadrans, all made of copper, and the silver denarius. The first three of the coins are the ones called "farthings" in the Bible. Among the understandable errors in the King James version of the Bible is the use of English coin denominations to describe ancient coins. Such is the case with the farthing. Some have argued that the farthing is the same as the lepton. If we go to the Greek text, however, we see it refers to the farthing denomination as an assarion and once as a kodrantes or quadrans.

"Are not two sparrows sold for a farthing?" (Matthew 10: 29)

"Verily I say unto thee, thou shalt by no means come out thence, till thou hast paid the uttermost farthing." (Matthew 5: 26)

"Are not five sparrows sold for two farthings, and not one of them is forgotten before God?" (Luke 12: 6)

The Greek text uses the words two assaria. A dupondius was equal to two asses. Madden attributes the coins referred to here to the island of Chios which actually had "assarion" engraved on them, but they could have been any contemporary issues, either Roman or colonial.

The quadrans was a quarter of an as. Some researchers feel that the coin mentioned in the references above were actually the bronze coins of that denomination struck at Antioch and which were abundant in circulation.

The Silver Denarius (Penny)

This is the most frequently named coin in the New Testament.

"But the same servant went out, and found one of his fellow servants, which owed him a hundred pence: and he laid hands on him, and took him by the throat, saying, Pay me that thou owest." (Matthew 18: 28)

"And when he had agreed with the labourers for a penny a day, he sent them into his vineyard." (Matthew 20: 2)

"... And they say unto him, Shall we go and but two hundred pennyworth of bread, and give them to eat?" (Mark 6: 37; See also John 6: 7)

"Why was not this ointment sold for three hundred pence and given to the poor?" (John 12: 5; See also Mark 14: 5)

The first silver denarius with what seems to be a reference to the Holy Land was minted soon after Pompey's victory in 55 B.C. It is a silver denarius of the Roman Republic struck by moneyer A. Plautius Aed.Cur. The obverse shows a turreted head of Cybele and is unremarkable for our purposes. The reverse, according to Crawford, refers to the surrender of an eastern ruler in the course of Pompey's campaigns.

The design tells the story: a camel is standing with its reins held by a kneeling figure holding an olive branch in his left hand. The legend is Bacchius Iudaeus, (Bacchus the Jew). There is dispute over the actual meaning of this, but one theory is that it is evidence of the assimilation of the Jewish culture into the Roman one.

There is no coin more familiar to readers of the Bible than the Tribute Penny.

"... Is it lawful to give tribute to Caesar, or not? Shall we give, or shall we not give? But He, knowing their hypocrisy, said unto them, Why tempt ye me? bring me a penny that I may see it. And they brought it. And he saith unto them, Whose is this image and superscription? And they said unto him, Caesar's. And Jesus answering said unto them, Render to Caesar the things that are Caesar's and to God the things that are God's. And they marvelled at him." (Mark 12: 14-17; See also Matthew 22: 19; Luke 20: 24).

Tiberius, A.D. 14-37
Denarius, 14-mid 20's

"There was a certain creditor which had two debtors: the one owed five hundred pence and the other fifty." (Luke 7: 41)

"And on the morrow when he departed, he took out two pence, and gave them to the host, and said unto him, Take care of him; and whatsoever thou spendest more, when I come again, I will repay thee." (Luke 10: 35)

"... A measure of wheat for a penny, and three measures of barley for a penny." (Revelation 6: 6)

Even without a coin to memorialize it, Jesus' manifestation of the inviolability of the separation of church and state was inspiring and is something all Americans, starting with the framers of our Constitution, have held dear. The penny, of course, was without a doubt really a denarius. This standard silver coin of Rome followed the expansion of the Empire. The New Testament calls it a "penny" because the silver denarius became the silver denar in medieval Europe and eventually became part of the English coinage system, where it evolved into the silver penny and later into a copper version. For as long as the penny was in use, until 1971, its symbol was the letter "d."

The coin shown to Jesus could only have been a denarius of Emperor Tiberius, who issued only one basic type during his thirty-three year reign. His laureate bust is on the obverse while the reverse shows his mother Livia (symbolizing Pax, the goddess of peace) seated, holding an olive branch and sceptre.

Tribute or tax? For whom?

It is important to recognize that there were two forms of tribute money, one sacred the other civil. The sacred tribute has a long history in scripture. Exodus (30: 13,16 and 38: 26) concerns the payment of half a shekel as "atonement money" by every male aged twenty or over:

"This they shall give, every one that passeth among them that are numbered, half a shekel after the shekel of the sanctuary;... an half shekel shall be the offering unto the Lord. and A bekah for every man, that is, half a shekel after the shekel of the sanctuary, for every one that went to be numbered, from twenty years old and upward, for six hundred thousand and three thousand and five hundred and fifty men."

In other words, not only was this a tax, it was also a census.

Under Joash (2 Chronicles 24: 4-14) it was stipulated that this was the amount to be collected annually for Temple repairs.

"And they made a proclamation throughout Judah and Jerusalem, to bring in to the Lord the collection that Moses the servant of God laid upon Israel in the wilderness."

Nehemiah (10: 32) informs us. *"Also we made ordinances for us, to charge ourselves yearly with the third part of a shekel for the service of the house of our God."* In other words, after the return from captivity, this became the voluntary annual payment. The amount reverted to a half shekel with the Diaspora when the Jews were dispersed throughout the world but continued to pay towards the Temple.

ROMAN COINS AND THE HOLY LAND

There is a well-known passage in the Book of Matthew (17: 24-27) concerning tribute money:

"And when they came to Capernaum they that had received tribute money came to Peter, and said, Doth not your master pay tribute?

He saith, Yes. And when he has come into the house, Jesus prevented him, saying, What thinkest thou, Simon? of whom do the kings of the earth take custom or tribute? of their own children or of strangers?

Peter saith unto him, Of strangers. Jesus saith unto him, Then are the children free.

Notwithstanding, lest we should offend them, go thou to the sea, and cast a hook, and take up the fish that first cometh up; and when thou has opened his mouth, thou shalt find a piece of money; that take, and give unto them, for me and thee."

This was another sacred tribute and the amount of the tax in Greek was a didrachm, the equivalent of half a shekel. The tax for two people would have been four drachms (a tetradrachm), the actual value of the coin in the fish.

The other kind of tribute was a civil tax collected by the publicans on goods at bridges, gates and harbors, similar to what we would call a toll or a customs duty today: *"Render therefore to all their dues: tribute to whom tribute is due, custom to whom custom; fear to whom fear; honor to whom honor. Romans."* (Romans 13: 7)

There was also a poll tax that was payable to the Emperor of Rome when Judea became a province: *"And it came to pass in those days that there went out a decree from Caesar Augustus that all the world should be taxed. Since everyone had to be taxed in the city of their birth, so Joseph and Mary went from Nazareth to Bethlehem."* (Luke 2: 1)

Vespasian fixed the tax at a didrachm (or two denarii) a head. After the First Revolt, the tribute for the "captive Jews" was designated to pay for the temple of Jupiter, which the Romans built atop the ruins of the Holy Temple. This is the same tax of which the revocation was celebrated with a coin by Emperor Nerva.

THE JUDEA CAPTA COINAGE

The Judea Capta Coinage

Although it can be argued that the first Judea Capta issue was a A.D. 69 sestertius of Vitellius as it shows Victory in the same poses as on later issues, the first coins that specifically mention Judea were struck by Vespasian after the victory in A.D. 70. This was the first important event of Vespasian's reign and probably the one with the most long-term significance. After the destruction of the Temple, it was memorialized for eternity architecturally and numismatically.

The Arch of Titus near the Coliseum, at the southeast corner in Rome vividly portrays the sacking of the Temple, with the Romans carrying away the Menorah and the showbread table with the omer-cup on top. Coins were issued by Vespasian (A.D. 69-79), Titus (A.D. 79-81) and even Domitian (A.D. 81-96), who personally had nothing to do with it. Coins were issued in all metals, gold, silver, and bronze, and may be classified into two groups, those specifically identifying the event with wording such as IVDEA, IVDEA CAPTA, DE IVDAEIS,IVDEA DEVICTA, IVDAEA NAVALIS, and those without the wording but nonetheless referring to the event through their symbolism.

The usual reverse types encountered among coins in the first category are (with variations in embellishments, positions, and placement):

1) Jewess seated on ground before trophy.

Vespasian, A.D. 69-79
Denarius

2) Jewess with hands bound seated on ground before palm tree.

Vespasian, Dupondius

3) As above, with a soldier standing behind.

Vespasian, A.D. 71
Sestertius

4) Jewess with hands bound standing before a palm tree.

5) A palm tree with a Jew standing to its left, hands tied behind his back; at right, a Jewess seated and weeping.

Vespasian,
Sestertius

6) Helmet, shield, and breastplate next to palm tree with Jewess seated at right.

Titus Caesar, A.D. 72-73
Aureus

7) Emperor in military garb standing to left of palm tree; seated Jewess at right.

Vespasian,
Sestertius

8) Victory standing, inscribing the letters S.P.Q.R. ("the Senate and people of Rome") or the Emperor's name on a shield attached to a palm tree; Jewess seated on ground at right.

Vespasian,
Sestertius

9) A trophy made up of helmet, breastplate, spear and shields.

10) Victory standing on a galley's prow.

As of Titus

There are coins in the second category with similar designs to those above but without any wording in the legend specific to Judea. Nonetheless, the design is specific enough to this series that they clearly belong to it.

Vespasian, A.D. 75-79
Gold Quinarius

88

Other types include the Emperor in or beside a triumphal quadriga leading captured prisoners, captive(s) kneeling, and Emperor on horseback spearing a foe. Rev. Edgar Rogers suggests that coins of these emperors with a Capricorn refer to the Judean conquest because astrologers believed "Capricorn is the sign which governs the Hebrew race." It is more likely, however, according to Sydenham, that these coins are homage to the Golden Age of Augustus.

The Judea Capta coins, which have received most of the attention, have been the ones struck in Rome to imperial specifications, but there were a good number of small and medium bronze coins struck in Caesaraea also, with legends in Greek and mostly portraying Victory standing with either a palm tree or a captive Jew.

The Judea Capta Issues of Caesarea Assarion, A.D. 71-73

Titus Caesar, A.D. 72-73 Two Assaria

The Tax Repeal Coin of Nerva (A.D. 96-98)

Imagine, if you will, the scene if the President of the United States 1) told the Internal Revenue Service that it needed to treat people better when trying to collect taxes, and then 2) instructed the United States Mint to issue a commemorative coin in honor of his doing so.

Emperor Nerva did precisely that. As we saw earlier, when Rome fell to Vesapasian and Titus, the didrachm that had been collected for the Temple tax was redirected to support the newly constructed temple of Jupiter Capitolinus and was called the Fiscus Judaicus. During the reign of Domitian, the tax was enforced with inquisitorial, malicious, and humiliating vengeance and false accusation (calumnia).

Nerva Tax

A look at the last word ("sublata") in the legend on the large bronze sestertius FISCI.IVDAICI.CALUMNIA.SUBLATA would lead one to think that the tax had been abolished. Records have been found though, which show that the tax was still being paid in later years. What actually happened was that the tax itself was not revoked, only the methods used to collect it. From then on, anyone who did not admit to being Jewish was exempted from the tax and was no longer included on the Jewish tax rolls. The tax itself remained in effect until near the end of the Roman Empire.

Hadrian's Visit and Aelia Capitolina

During the middle years of his reign (c. A.D. 120-134), Hadrian was so preoccupied with visiting the provinces of his realm that he was seldom seen in Rome. The motives for such extensive travel remain uncertain, but probably have something to do with an inquisitive mind and a desire to bring some unity and cohesion to the Empire. There are a large number of coins chronicling his journeys which conform to four specific types: a type personifying the province by its design; the Adventus type showing Hadrian standing extending his arm towards a figure representing the province, the Restitutor type in which Hadrian is raising the figure, and the Exercitus type showing the Emperor on horseback.

For Judea we know examples of the first two types. On the first coin, Hadrian is standing as described facing a female (Judea). She is holding a box and a patera over a knee-high altar. A bull to be sacrificed is between them as are two children holding raised palm branches.

Hadrian Adventus

The second coin, the "adventus" type, has the same figures without the bull, and the children are seen standing on either side of Judea.

These coins were issued in A.D. 131-132, before the Bar-Kochba War but most likely after Hadrian ordered the establishment of a colony at Jerusalem. The city of Aelia Capitolina was established before the war, thought it is uncertain when it was completed. There are no known coins of Roman origin but a good number of colonial issues making reference to Aelia Capitolina. The legend is usually a variant of C A C, COL. AEL. or CAP. There are a number of interesting reverse types including Hadrian plowing the fields of the city he just founded and especially a representation of the temple of Jupiter Capitolina within which Jupiter is seated between the standing figures of Pallas and the Genius of the city. Coins were minted in the new city through the reign of Herennius Etruscus and Hostilian in A.D. 251. The coins struck after that in Jerusalem were by the conquering Arabs.

*The Coinage of Aelia Capitolina
Roman City of Jerusalem*

*The Coinage of Aelia Capitolina
Roman City of Jerusalem*

COINS AND CHRISTIANITY

COINS AND CHRISTIANITY

There are a few coins that have nothing to do with the Bible and nothing to do with the Holy Land, but which still deserve mention. First among them are the coins of Constantine the Great (A.D. 307-337), who is recognized as the first Christian Emperor of Rome as a result of his deathbed conversion. Before that, he gave some evidence of his acceptance of a new deity after his victory in battle over Maxentius when he altered the labarum, the Emperor's standard when he was with the army. He added to it the Greek letters chi and rho (XP), the monogram of Christ with an alpha and an omega on either side, symbolic of the beginning and the end. This "christogram" would become a common component of the reverse on the coins of Constantine's successors. Most of Constantine's coins provide only scant evidence of any acceptance of Christianity and instead ratified his earlier pagan beliefs, but in about A.D. 314 there were several interesting numismatic developments.

*Jovian,
A.D. 363-364
Solidus*

Constantine issued some coins commemorating his predecessors Claudius II, Constantius Chlorus and Maximian Herculius on which he disallowed the depiction of pagan rites on their reverses. Also in 314, the Tarragona mint used the cross as a coin device. A little later, two Christian monograms are found on the Emperor's helmet on some coins struck at Scissia, the mint of Upper Pannonia. It was a number of years, however, before Constantine's successors institutionalized the new state religion on its coins.

*Justinian II,
Second Reign,
A.D. 705-711,
Solidus*

III

COINS AND CHRISTIANITY

When the Roman Empire was split in two, the one in the west slowly died while the one in the east with Byzantium (Istanbul) as its capital and now known as the Byzantine Empire, continued the Roman heritage but with the Christian religion. Justinian II became emperor in A.D. 685 and soon put the figure of Christ on his coins where he is shown holding the Gospel in one hand and offering a blessing. The inscription around reads Rex Regnatum (King of Kings).

Christ next appeared on coins in a very large series of anonymous (without the name of a ruler) bronze issues struck from roughly A.D. 969 to 1118. These coins, which are common even today, have Jesus on the obverse in various poses. One issue also has the Virgin Mary on the reverse.

The first representation of the Virgin Mary on a coin occurred during the reign of Leo VI (A.D. 886-912), where she is shown offering a prayer. Finally, the first of many images of the Virgin and child on a coin was initiated by John Zimisces from A.D. 969-976.

John I Tzimisces,
A.D. 969-976
Histamenon

TIME LINE

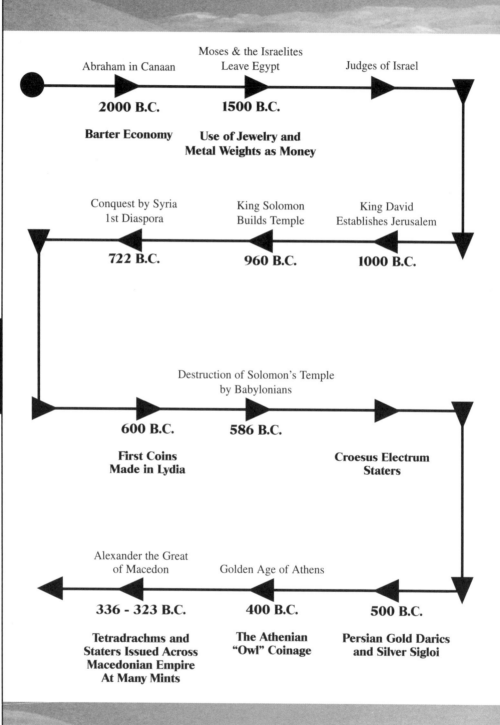

Abraham in Canaan

Moses & the Israelites
Leave Egypt

Judges of Israel

2000 B.C.

1500 B.C.

Barter Economy

**Use of Jewelry and
Metal Weights as Money**

Conquest by Syria
1st Diaspora

King Solomon
Builds Temple

King David
Establishes Jerusalem

722 B.C.

960 B.C.

1000 B.C.

Destruction of Solomon's Temple
by Babylonians

600 B.C.

586 B.C.

**First Coins
Made in Lydia**

**Croesus Electrum
Staters**

Alexander the Great
of Macedon

Golden Age of Athens

336 - 323 B.C.

400 B.C.

500 B.C.

**Tetradrachms and
Staters Issued Across
Macedonian Empire
At Many Mints**

**The Athenian
"Owl" Coinage**

**Persian Gold Darics
and Silver Sigloi**

TIME LINE

Beginning of Seleucid Era

Seleucids and Ptolemies of Egypt Vie For Control of Holy land Egyptian Control

Antiochus II Defeats Egypt

312 B.C.

300 B.C.

220 B.C.

**Ptolemaic Tetradrachms
Issued in Large Quantity
Same Style and Many Mints**

Syrians Give Simon Maccabaeus
Right of Coinage (unused)

Maccabean
Rededicate Temple

164 B.C.

200 B.C.

Seleucid Tetradrachms

John Hyrcanus I
1st Hasmonean Ruler

Alexander Jannaeus

135 B.C.

126 B.C. - A.D. 79

100 B.C.

First Leptons

Shekels of Tyre

**The Widow's Mite
(Lepton of
Alexander Jannaeus)**

Herodian Dynasty Begins
With Herod I
(The Great)

Pompey Leads Roman
Conquest
Installs John Hyrcanus II
Murder of Julius Caesar

37 B.C.

44 B.C.

63 B.C.

**Lepton of Herod I
With Helmet**

Ides Mar Dererius

Coin of Pompey

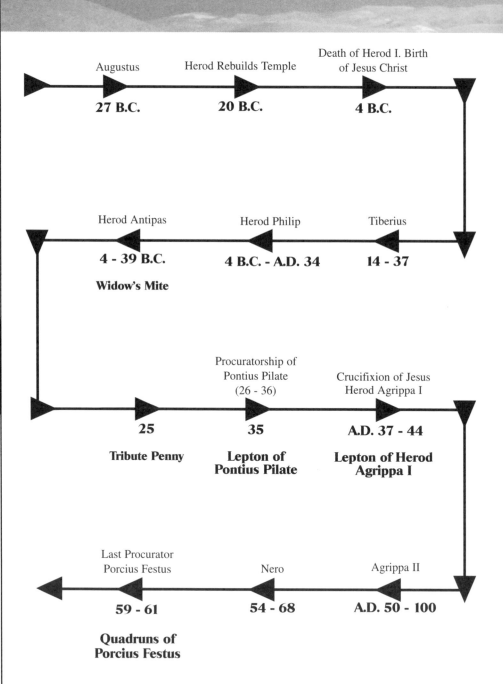

Augustus — 27 B.C.

Herod Rebuilds Temple — 20 B.C.

Death of Herod I. Birth of Jesus Christ — 4 B.C.

Herod Antipas — 4 - 39 B.C. — **Widow's Mite**

Herod Philip — 4 B.C. - A.D. 34

Tiberius — 14 - 37

25 — **Tribute Penny**

Procuratorship of Pontius Pilate (26 - 36) — 35 — **Lepton of Pontius Pilate**

Crucifixion of Jesus Herod Agrippa I — A.D. 37 - 44 — **Lepton of Herod Agrippa I**

Last Procurator Porcius Festus — 59 - 61 — **Quadruns of Porcius Festus**

Nero — 54 - 68

Agrippa II — A.D. 50 - 100

TIME LINE

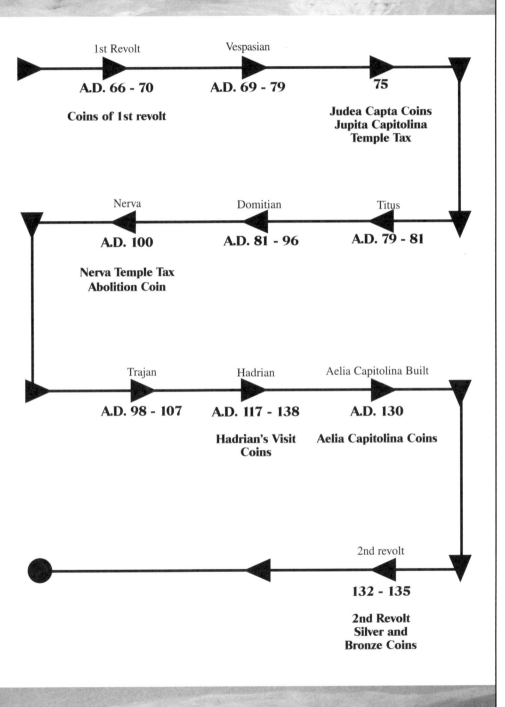

GLOSSARY

GLOSSARY

Alexander the Great (356-323 B.C.): Son of Phillip II of Macedon. Alexander's grand empire extended from Thrace to Egypt and from Greece to the Indus valley.

Alexander Jannaeus (103-76 B.C.): Ruled the Jewish people for 27 years. His reign was marked by territorial expansion and good times. He was the first Hasmonean ruler to style himself king on his coins and the first to use Greek for his name and title.

Antigonus Mattathias (40-37 B.C.): Last Hasmonean ruler of Judea, he was taken captive by Romans, imprisoned, and then beheaded.

Aramaic: A Semitic language similar to Hebrew and the main spoken language of the Holy Land.

Athens: Ancient city-state that produced great philosophers such as Plato and Aristotle. Exerted political influence throughout the ancient world.

Babylonia: Ancient cultural region occupying southeastern Mesopotamia between the Tigris and Euphrates Rivers. Present-day Iraq.

Barter: To trade by exchanging one commodity for another.

Canaan: Ancient region roughly corresponding to later Palestine.

Daric: Term used to describe a gold coin that was struck by authority of Darius, King of Persia.

Darius (522–486 B.C.): King of Persia.

Denarius: The standard silver coin of ancient Rome.

Diaspora: The dispersion of Jews among the Gentiles after the Babylonian exile.

Drachm: A Greek silver coin.

Electrum: A natural pale yellow alloy of gold and silver.

First Jewish Revolt (A.D. 66-70): First Jewish rebellion against Roman rule in Judea. Provoked by the desecration of the local synagogue by Hellenists. Ended when Roman troops under Titus captured Jerusalem.

Hadrian: Emperor who ruled Rome from 117-138 and sought to end distinctions between Rome and the Roman provinces.

GLOSSARY

Half shekel: A unit of value based on a weight of gold or silver.

Herod Agrippa I (c. 10 B.C. - A.D. 44): Grandson of Herod the Great. Became known as "Agrippa the Great."

Herod Agrippa II (A.D. 27- 93): Son of Herod Agrippa I and Cypros. Emperor Claudius appointed Agrippa several tetrarchies and the title of king. Nero gave him land in Galilee and Paraea.

Herod Antipas (21 B.C. - A. D. 39): Son of Herod the Great and Malthrace of Samaria. Tetrarch of Galilee.

Herod Archelaus (22 B.C. - A.D. 18): Became ruler of Judea when his father Herod the Great died. Known as Herod the Ethnarch.

Herod Philip (20 B.C. – A.D. 34): Son of Herod the Great. Tetrarch over the northern part of his father's kingdom.

Herod the Great (73-4 B.C.): Roman Mark Anthony appointed Herod to be King of Judea in 37 B.C.

John Hyrancus I (135-106 B.C): Son of Simon Maccabaeus. He was the first Jewish prince to have his name on his coins. Became High Priest of Jerusalem.

Josephus, or Josephus Flavius (A.D. 37-100): Jewish military leader who was captured by Romans during -the Jewish Revolt. He later became a historian. His works constitute a readily available source for the study of Jewish life of that period, though his accounts are not entirely reliable.

Judea Capta Coins: Coins that were struck to commemorate the feat of the Jews at the hands of Titus in A.D. 70.

King David (c. 1004-965 B.C.): He established Israel as a major power in the region, united twelve Israeli tribes in one kingdom, and founded his capital in Jerusalem. King Solomon (c. 965-930 B.C.): Son of King David. He strengthened the kingdom and built the first Temple of Jerusalem.

Lepton: A small Judean bronze coins. Also a unit of currency in modern Greece.

Lydia: An ancient country of west-central Asia Minor on the Aegean Sea in present-day northwest Turkey.

Mt. Moriah: Site where the Temple of Jerusalem was built.

GLOSSARY

Nebuchadnezzar: King of Babylonia who took children of Judah to Babylon in 587 B.C.

Pontius Pilate: Succeeded Valerius Gratus in A.D. 26. He was Tiberius' governor and best known for delivering Jesus to be crucified.

Porcius Festus: Procurator of Judea for a year under Nero.

Procurator: An officer of the Roman Empire who managed financial affairs of a province and had administrative powers as agent of the emperor.

Prutah: A coin formerly used in Israel, equal to one thousandth of a pound.

Ptolemy: An Egyptian dynasty of (323-30 B.C.).

Regnal: Being a specified year of a monarch's reign calculated from the date of accession.

Second Jewish Revolt (A.D. 131-135): Revolt against Rome, led by Simon Bar-Kochba. Roman emperor Hadrian had promised to rebuild Jerusalem and the Temple, then changed his mind and decided to establish a Roman colony, and this ignited the revolt. The Romans leveled Jerusalem and exiled the population.

Seleucids: Member of a Greek dynasty that ruled Syria and other territories from 312 B.C. to 64 B.C.

Shekel: A unit of value based on a weight of gold or silver.

Siglos: Silver coin struck during the reign of Darius I of Persia and his successors.

Simon Bar-Kochba: The leader of the Second Jewish Revolt in A.D. 132.

Simon Maccabaeus: High Priest of Judea, who was granted by the Syrians the right to coin money, but who did not.

Staters: Coins first produced in Lydia. Became one of the standard denominations, especially for gold coins in the Greek world.

Syria: Ancient Syria included Lebanon, most of present-day Israel and Jordan, and part of Iraq and Saudia Arabia. Settled c. 2100 B.C. by Amorites. the region was later conquered by Hittites, Assyrians, Babylonians, Persians, Greeks, and Romans.

Tetradrachm: Standard large silver coin of the Greek world equal to four drachms.

GLOSSARY

The First Temple of Jerusalem: It was built by King Solomon around 950 B.C. and was a center of Jewish religious life. It united the people of Israel until its destruction by the Babylonian king Nebuchadnezzar.

The Second Temple of Jerusalem: Built by Jews returning from the Babylon Exile in 517 B.C. It was destroyed by the Romans in A.D. 70.

Tiberius (42 B.C. – A.D. 37): Chosen by Augustus to be heir to the throne. Tiberius ruled Rome from A.D. 14-37.

Tribute Penny: A Roman denarius of the Emperor Tiberius.

Tyre: Ancient Phoenician city on the eastern Mediterranean Sea in present-day southern Lebanon.

Vespasian (A.D. 9-79): A soldier who helped squelch the First Jewish Revolt. He became emperor of Rome when Nero died in A.D. 69.

Widow's Mite: Smallest Judean bronze coin, more properly called a lepton.

BIBLIOGRAPHY

Ackerman, John Yonge, *Numismatic Illustrations of the Narrative Portions of the New Testament.* London: John Russell Smith, 1846.

Avi-Yonah, Michael, ed., *A History of Israel and the Holy Land.* Jerusalem: Jerusalem Publishing House, 2001.

Banks, Florence Aiken, *Coins of Bible Days.* New York: MacMillan Publishing, 1955.

Burnett, Andrew, *Interpreting the Past* – Coins. London: British Museum Press, 1991.

Clain-Stefanelli, Elvira and Vladimir, *The Beauty and Lore of Coins, Currency and Medals.* Croton on Hudson: NY, Riverwood Publishers, 1974.

Crawford, M.H., *Roman Republican Coinage.* Cambridge: Cambridge UP, 1974.

Dudley, Donald R. *The Romans*, 850 B.C. – A.D. 37. New York: Alfred A Knopf, 1970.

Grun, Bernard, *The Timetables of History.* New York: Simon & Schuster, 1979.

Halliday, G.R., *Money Talks About the Bible.* Hollywood, CA: G.R. Halliday, 1948.

Head, Barclay V., *Historia Numorum, A Manual of Greek Numismatics.* Oxford: Clarendon P, 1911.

Hendin, David, *Guide to Biblical Coins.* 4th ed. Nyack, NY: Amphora Books, 2001.

Hill, George Francis, *A Catalogue of Greek Coins in the British Museum. A Catalog of the Greek Coins of Palestine, Galilee, Samaria and Judea.* London: The British Museum, 1914.

Hill, George Francis, *A Catalogue of Greek Coins in the British Museum. A Catalog of the Greek Coins of Phoenicia.* London: The British Museum, 1910.

Hill, George Francis, *Handbook of Ancient Greek and Roman Coins.* 1899. Chicago: Argonaut , 1964.

Jenkins, G.K., *Ancient Greek Coins.* New York: G.P. Putnam's Sons, 1972.

Josephus, *The Jewish War.* Trans. by G.A. Williamson. Rev. by E. Mary Smallwood. London: Penguin Books, 1981.

Leu Numismatics. Auction Catalogs. Zurich, 2003-2004.

Lot, Ferdinand, *The End of the Ancient World and the Beginning of the Middle Ages.* New York: Harper & Row, 1961.

BIBLIOGRAPHY

Madden, Frederic C. *History of Jewish Coinage*, 1864. San Diego: Pegasus, 1967.

Mattingly, Harold, *Roman Coins from the Earliest Times to the Fall of the Western Empire*. 2nd ed. London, Chicago: Quadrangle Books, 1960.

Meshorer, Ya'akov, *A Treasury of Jewish Coins*. Jerusalem and Nyack, NY: Yad Ben Zvi P & Amphora Books, 2001.

Rogers, Edgar, *Handy Guide to Jewish Coins*. (London, 1914. Reprint Rockville Center, Sanford J. Durst, NY, 2001.

Romanoff, Paul, Jewish Symbols on Ancient Jewish Coins. 1944. New York: American Israel Numismatic Association, 1971.

Samuels, Claudia Wallach, Paul Rynearson and Ya'akov Meshorer, *The Numismatic Legacy of the Jews as Depicted by a Distinguished American Collection.* New York: Stack's, 2000.

Seltman, Charles, *Greek Coins*. 2nd ed. London: Methuen, 1955.

Starr, Chester G., *A History of the Ancient World*. New York: Oxford U P, 1965.

Starr, Chester G., *Civilization and the Caesars. The Intellectual Revolution in the Roman Empire*. New York: W.W. Norton & Co., Inc., 1954.

Sutherland, C.H.V., *Roman Coins*, London: Barrie & Jenkins, 1974.

Sydenham, Edward F., Historical References on Coins of the Roman Empire from Augustus to Gallienius. Reprint of 1917 ed. London and San Diego, Spink & Son, Ltd., & Pegasus Publishing Co., 1968.

Uris, Leon, *Jerusalem*. Garden City, NY: Doubleday, 1981.

Whiting, P.D., *Byzantine Coins*. New York: G.P. Putnam's Sons, 1973.

Wirgin, Wolf and Siegfried Mandel, *The History of Coins and Symbols in Ancient Israel*. New York: Exposition P, 1958.

Yeoman, Richard S., *Moneys of the Bible*, Racine, WI: Whitman Publishing, 1961.

Zondervaan Handbook to the Bible, Grand Rapids, MI: Zondervaan, 1999.

ARTHUR L. FRIEDBERG

Arthur L. Friedberg, B.A., M.B.A., has been a professional numismatist for over thirty years. He has been a member of the prestigious Professional Numismatists Guild since 1977, and his firm, The Coin & Currency Institute, Inc. is a founding member of the elite International Association of Professional Numismatists (I.A.P.N.). In 2001 he was elected President of the Association, marking the first time in the fifty-year history of the organization that an American has occupied the office. He is also a life member of the American Numismatic Association.

Friedberg joined Coin & Currency (a family firm) in 1972 after receiving his Bachelor of Arts degree in history from The George Washington University in Washington, D.C. He then earned a Master of Business Administration degree with emphasis in management and marketing from New York University in 1976. Within a short period of time, he co-authored with his brother, Ira, revisions of Gold Coins of the World (now in its 7th edition) and Paper Money of the United States (now in its 17th edition).

The seventh edition of Gold Coins of the World was five years in the making and marks the book's 45th anniversary as the standard reference work on the subject. Since its first appearance in 1958, subsequent editions appeared in 1965, 1971, 1976, 1980, and 1992. Today's book bears little resemblance to its ancestors, having been adapted to present-day standards. In 1993 it was awarded the Prix d'Honneur of the I.A.P.N. as the best book of the preceding year.

Friedberg wrote the new edition of Appraising and Selling Your Coins, the 24th edition, which was released in 1996 by a division of Random House, and which has more than a quarter of a million copies in print. He also published and edited the revisions to R.S. Yeoman's classics, Modern World Coins and Current Coins of the World. He is a contributor to the Standard Catalog of World Coins and has written numerous articles for Numismatist, the journal of the American Numismatic Association.

Friedberg was awarded the Medal of Merit of the American Numismatic Association (1992) for "distinguished service to the hobby," the first place Heath Literary Award (1994) for the article judged best in Numismatist during 1993, and the Swiss Vrenelli Prize (1999) for "outstanding contributions to numismatics."

In addition to writing, publishing, and general numismatic activities, he often serves as an expert on the coin business and on United States and foreign coins and paper money for some of America's leading law firms and insurers and has been a member of the Panel of Arbitrators of the American Arbitration Association.